Arthur Silva White

Britannic Confederation

A series of papers

Arthur Silva White

Britannic Confederation
A series of papers

ISBN/EAN: 9783337182571

Printed in Europe, USA, Canada, Australia, Japan

Cover: Foto ©ninafisch / pixelio.de

More available books at **www.hansebooks.com**

BRITANNIC CONFEDERATION.

BRITANNIC CONFEDERATION.

A Series of Papers by

ADMIRAL SIR JOHN COLOMB,
PROFESSOR EDWARD A. FREEMAN,
GEORGE G. CHISHOLM,
PROFESSOR SHIELD NICHOLSON,
MAURICE H. HERVEY,

AND

THE RIGHT HONBLE. LORD THRING.

EDITED, WITH AN INTRODUCTION, BY

ARTHUR SILVA WHITE,

SECRETARY AND EDITOR, ROYAL SCOTTISH GEOGRAPHICAL SOCIETY.

Published by the
Authority of the Council of the Royal Scottish Geographical Society.
Reprinted from the " Scottish Geographical Magazine."

With a New Map of the British Empire.

LONDON:

GEORGE PHILIP & SON, 32 FLEET STREET, E.C.;

LIVERPOOL: 45 TO 51 SOUTH CASTLE STREET.

1892.

CONTENTS.

MAP AND DIAGRAMS.

MAP OF THE BRITISH EMPIRE, AND ITS OFFICIAL
AND COMMERCIAL RELATIONS.

DIAGRAMS TO MR. CHISHOLM'S PAPER.

INTRODUCTION.

THE present series of papers was planned with the object of partly satisfying the recent public demand for clearer and more reasonable views concerning the question of Imperial Federation. These papers were originally published in the *Scottish Geographical Magazine*—the Monthly Journal of the Royal Scottish Geographical Society—and are now re-issued in book-form, in order to meet the demand for a wider circulation.

The intention of the Series is to treat the subject academically, as being one for legitimate discussion by students of Applied Geography. Although necessarily limited to those aspects which came more or less within their horizon, a considerable amount of latitude has been allowed to the authors of the papers, who have not hesitated to avail themselves of this freedom of treatment. Indeed, the reader cannot fail to observe a good deal of adverse criticism. Most of the vital points at issue have consequently been examined in greater or less detail, in accordance with the judgment of individual contributors; and, it is to be hoped, the ground has thereby been cleared for a rational and profitable discussion of the whole question. They have dealt with facts, and not with fancies.

The contributors alone are responsible for their respective statements.

A map of the British Empire has been specially constructed to illustrate this series of papers. It was designed by myself, and compiled by Mr. J. G. Bartholomew. An attempt has been made to indicate the official and commercial relations between the British Empire and foreign countries by a system of lettering and colouring which is readily discernible. Extraneous data are rigidly excluded.

It is doubtless a misfortune that no name can, apparently, be found to characterise the closer and more permanent union which, in the opinion of the Federationists, should replace the ill-defined and unstable relations existing at the present day between Great Britain and her Colonies. But, after all, it is not so much the *name* as the *thing* which is of prime importance. There will be time enough to find a more appropriate designation when once the component parts of the British Empire have been consolidated into a responsible World-power. At present, we are only groping in the dark towards the attainment of an ideal on which history sheds little or no light.

The title selected for this series of papers is, therefore, not free from objection; but at least it has the merit of implying an inviolable political union between those self-governing Colonies which at the present time acknowledge the over-rule of Her Britannic Majesty.

It is assumed, in the absence of any matured scheme, that this union, which exists already in theory rather than in fact, will take the form of a Confederation. Obviously, too, all Crown Dependencies are excluded.

During the year 1891 the great Colonies made considerable progress in the direction of Britannic Confederation. It is clear that, before a scheme of sufficient elasticity can be found to bind the self-governing Colonies together, and attach them to the British Crown by ties which should bear any ordinary friction, the political unity of adjacent Colonies is an essential condition of success. Geographically speaking, territories under the same—or approximately the same—conditions of economical productiveness, demand and supply, gain immeasurably in strength if they can present to the outside world an united front, and to each other perfect freedom of intercommunication and interchange of commodities. Thus, the separate Colonies of Australasia have found no difficulty in adopting, at least in principle, a plan of Federation among themselves on Free Trade lines. Their attitude towards the Empire has been sufficiently characterised by the maintenance, at their own expense, of an Auxiliary Squadron of the Imperial Navy in Australian waters. Since this community of interests has been recognised, is it too much to hope that the obstacles to Britannic Confederation will not be found to be insuperable ?

Unfortunately, the very reverse of these conditions is observable in the North American continent, where the Colony of Newfoundland and the Dominion of Canada have been unable to agree upon the Fisheries Question, and have in consequence displayed a lamentable want of unity of interests. But in this case the proximity of a foreign State has complicated, if not caused, this divergence of interests. It is an exception to our case which proves the rule. Fortunately, the loyalty of the powerful and prosperous Dominion of Canada to the Imperial connection has survived a severe test. Although, as every geographer must concede, the political destinies of Canada are intimately associated with the development of the whole North American continent, they are not of necessity exclusively dependent thereon. The result of the recent general election in Canada expressed the determination of the Dominion to cast in its lot with Great Britain, and thus to maintain its political unity, rather than to relinquish its independence by the alternative of absorption into the United States. Furthermore, by the completion of the Canadian Pacific Railway, and other public works, the greatest service has been rendered in the consolidation of the British Empire. Nor must it be overlooked that, both in Canada and Australia, the principles of Free Trade are rapidly gaining ground; for it is to the general adoption of these principles that the Empire must look for its ultimate consolidation.

In South Africa the movement in favour of Federation has made marked progress. But the unsettled political conditions, the presence of progressive Dutch States, and a preponderating native population, must necessarily delay the formulation of any practicable scheme. It is, however, to be noted that, in South Africa, a *Zollverein* has been advocated as the basis of any future political federation.

The recent commercial treaties concluded between the Allied Powers of Central Europe, being based on Free Trade principles, illustrate in a very striking manner what may be called the centripetal tendency of the economical interests of States, though, in the case of these Powers, their common action was, doubtless, largely inspired by motives of State policy.

If it be expedient for individual States thus to adjust the balance of power in continents, it is absolutely necessary for a World-power like Great Britain to provide against any disturbance of her vast Colonial relations. The loss of one or more of her great Colonies would, at the present stage in the World's history, be all but irretrievable ; and yet, by having conceded self-government to these Colonies, it is admitted that, in principle, she has revoked all claims of sovereignty over them : at least, a Colonial civil war is entirely out of the question. It is, therefore, quite natural that, in view of the possible disintegration of the Empire, no means should be left untried to bind its separate parts together by the strongest ties of political union.

Another danger which threatens the integrity of the Empire is the possibility of attack by a hostile Power. Probably this outweighs every other consideration, in so far as the immediate safety of the Empire is concerned : for to be prepared for war is to avert it. It is, therefore, reasonable to assume that the first important

step towards Britannic Confederation will be the formation of a League for Defence. The Colonial Empire of
Great Britain occupies the best strategic positions in
nearly every quarter of the World, and the possession
of any portion of it by a foreign Power would be
a constant menace to the safety of its other parts.
Granted that it be possible to establish a Britannic
Confederation capable of defending its vital interests
against any probable combination of Powers, its consolidation would be a mere matter of time. Even at the
present rate of growth of the Empire, and of its moral
and material progress, the time would not be long before
its members would enjoy the most enviable lot of any
nationality on Earth.

Moreover, the centre of gravity—so to speak—of
World-power is shifting constantly to the West. What
the Mediterranean Sea was before the discovery of
America, the Atlantic is to us to-day: the centre around
which are grouped the most advanced nations of the
Earth—the focus of civilisation. It is not too much to
infer that, once the Isthmus of Panama is cut, or otherwise ceases to offer obstacles to shipping, the stream of
human progress will partly become diverted into the
Pacific, and that the political development of the States
on its shores will receive an impulse such as the World
has never before experienced. An entirely new set of
political and commercial conditions will, of course, be a
necessary corollary to such a development: the Pacific
will then vie with the Atlantic for the supremacy in
human interests.

That, under these circumstances, the Colonial Empire of Great Britain, once consolidated, would exercise a preponderating influence on the World's history requires no further demonstration. If, indeed, it be found possible to achieve only a measure of this result, no degree of self-sacrifice, either on the part of the Colonies or on that of the mother-country, should be regarded as excessive.

ARTHUR SILVA WHITE.

EDINBURGH, 1st *February*, 1892.

I.

A SURVEY OF EXISTING CONDITIONS.

By Admiral Sir JOHN COLOMB, K.C.M.G., M.P.

A

POLITICAL terminology is generally difficult, but the title that has been selected for the series of papers to which the present one is introductory is more than usually free from objection. The substantive is well chosen, because the federal union to be attained in the scattered Empire of the Queen must necessarily assume the looser form of a confederacy, and not that of a federation, strictly so called. The adjective is equally apt, since " British " is so constantly used in the narrower, insular sense, whilst " Britannic " —the territorial title of the sovereign of these realms, who is to all the World " Her Britannic Majesty "—has a wider range of association, and fitly expresses the larger sweep of the idea it is desired to emphasise. If it be not too late to change, the Imperial Federation League might with advantage adopt the title of this series of papers.

To answer the question, " What is the empire of Her Britannic Majesty ?" we must turn first to geography and then to history. Geographically, the first thing noticeable is the scattered character of the Empire that is usually coloured red on the maps. It literally encircles the globe east and west, north and south. If it were not so scattered the first thing to strike the eye would be its vast extent,—more than nine millions of square miles of the Earth's surface, a fifth part of the

whole habitable globe, the largest empire of the ancient
or modern World. These characteristics lie patent.
But, if we begin to look closely and to analyse, two
other features shape themselves that have important
bearings. One of these is the distribution of the territories between the Temperate and the Torrid zones;
the other the isolated portion of the little land that
gives its name to, and is the political centre of, this
world-embracing Empire.

Of these characteristics the scattered position of the
component parts of the Empire and their climatological
distribution are the two that have the most direct
bearing on the present subject. The distribution of the
territories between Temperate and Tropical climates
enables us to draw a sharp line between the Tropical
and the Temperate countries. The political confederation of the Empire can refer only to those countries
where men of British race live from one generation to
another under free British political institutions. Whatever the more remote future may have in store, the
present question must leave out of account those Tropical portions of the Empire inhabited, and only capable
of permanent habitation, by the dark-skinned races,
governed by the vicegerents of Her Britannic Majesty,
and not intrusted with the free Briton's right of self-
government, still less therefore to be endowed with the
privilege of sharing in the government of other men
of British race. The only point of the question that
affects them is whether they would continue to be
governed by the United Kingdom alone, or by a united
empire. When we talk, then, of a Britannic confederation, we must really be thinking of the Britannic Empire
lying in Temperate or sub-Tropical latitudes; and that,

for practical purposes, at the present time resolves
itself into the United Kingdom of Great Britain and
Ireland, British North America, British South Africa,
and Australasia.

The second of the two characteristics having a direct
political bearing on our subject—the scattered position
of the four great groups just enumerated—is fundament-
ally responsible for the existence of such a question at
all as that which now confronts us. If these countries,
inhabited as they are by a population almost entirely
of common origin and otherwise homogeneous, had lain
in geographical contiguity, there would never have arisen
such a condition of affairs as we see at present in
the political relations of each part of the whole to the
centre and to the parts.   There might, indeed, and,
among a people so wedded to self-government in local
affairs, no doubt would have arisen, the need for some
loosening of the central authority over such matters by
the adoption of a federal system.   But the need for
drawing closer would never have occurred, because the
existing absence of almost every substantial political
tie would never have resulted under such geographical
conditions.   It is distance that has produced this result.
When the Colonies in the Temperate latitudes, inhabited by Britons, grew out of being governed on the
same principles as those in the Tropics, as mere dependencies of Great Britain, it was their distance from the
seat of government that prevented their incorporation
into the United Kingdom, or a legislative union being
thought of, while, as to the federal idea, it was not
until recently that it has come to be regarded by us as
a *via media* between complete legislative union and the
absence of all real political union whatever.   There

were undoubtedly other causes determining the direction that Colonial self-government then took. But, if the Colonies had been newly-opened countries next door to us, those causes themselves would never have been called into existence. It was geographical position that lay at the root of the developments that have taken place.

Historically, the actual course of events has been briefly this. All colonies and plantations having originally been treated alike—that is, both nursed and governed by Britain and from Britain—those that lay in Temperate regions, and had no native population of which any account had to be taken, but were inhabited entirely by men of British origin, became Little Britains, and after a time claimed the same amount of political freedom and the same political institutions as were enjoyed by their brethren in the mother-country. Distance making legislative union impossible, and federation not being "in the air," this political freedom was conferred by creating local Parliaments, and placing them in the same position towards the Crown, represented by the governor, as that held towards it directly by the Parliament of the United Kingdom. Nominally the Parliament of the United Kingdom as well as the Crown retained supreme authority over the Parliaments so constituted. Practically the power of the Parliament is a reserve force to be called out of abeyance only in great emergencies such as that which, while we write, has arisen with regard to Newfoundland; while that of the Crown, acting through the executive government of the United Kingdom (as distinguished from the Crown, represented by a colonial governor and acting through a colonial executive), is not much more substantial. The political connection between any Colony and the United Kingdom is of the slenderest; between any two Colonies, except where it has since been created—as between the Colonies of British North America by Canadian confederation—there is none at all.

But before we can get a complete bird's-eye view of the general situation we must note some other circumstances that accompanied the grant of parliamentary self-government to the Colonies. With the right to manage their own domestic affairs the government and people of the United Kingdom also made to the Colonists two free gifts of a strictly material nature, and at an enormous sacrifice to themselves not fully realised at the time. The first and greatest of these gifts was nothing less than the fee-simple of the vast territories, on the fringes of which they had settled.

The vastness of this unconditional and unreserved bounty is even now scarcely appreciated. The sacrifice it entailed on the mother-country is hardly recognised at all. It is not only that the heritage of the whole race was made over absolutely to a few mere handfuls of its members, so that now a native of Great Britain has no more property in and no more rights in or concerning the territory of Victoria, for instance, than any Frenchman or German possesses, and may even be refused permission to enter that territory if his pecuniary means fail to come up to a certain standard: that is not all. There was another and directly pecuniary sacrifice made when these lands were so lightly given away. The Empire of Great Britain has cost some eight hundred millions to build up. The National Debt was a mortgage upon the whole of the

territories composing that empire. Yet these large
and fertile lands, containing unknown reserves of
wealth, were simply given away to a few favoured
members of the race, freed from all responsibility for
the mortgage debt that lay upon them, the whole
burden of which remains on the shoulders of the
people of the United Kingdom. Nine-tenths and
more of the area of land charged with its repayment
has been released, and the whole stands secured upon
the remaining tenth.

After this it seems almost a small thing to come to
—but it was no small thing—the second pecuniary gift
that accompanied the concession of self-government to
the Colonies. The people of the United Kingdom
further gave them the right of levying all taxes, both
of customs and inland revenue, and applying the proceeds for their own exclusive benefit. And, negatively,
they required from them no contribution of any kind
whatever in respect of those Imperial services, supported
by the United Kingdom, of which the Colonists enjoyed the advantages especially with themselves.

These Imperial services consist of the naval and
military, the Diplomatic and Consular, and the Colonial
Office staff. The United Kingdom keeps up the
Colonial Office for the purpose of maintaining what may
be called the discipline of the Empire. For example,
Newfoundland was recently allowed to negotiate the
basis of a reciprocity treaty with the United States.
Canada objected that its terms were injurious to
her. The Colonial Office had to adjust these conflict-
ing interests; and we have lately read the kind of
language the Newfoundlanders use towards that Office
in consequence. It is by means of the first four-named

services that the foreign relations of the Empire, whether in peace or war, are conducted. These relations accordingly remain under the sole control of the Government and people of the United Kingdom. When, therefore, we speak of the political independence of the Colonies, there is this very large deduction to be made : that, whereas they are self-governing and mutually independent in respect of their domestic affairs, in respect of their foreign relations they remain, constitutionally, in as completely a dependent position as any of the Tropical Possessions of the Crown : and herein will be found to lie the whole *crux* of the matter. When the Colonies were granted the right of self-government, the grant was partial only ; they were not endowed with the Imperial franchise, because they were not then in a position to undertake the corresponding Imperial obligations and responsibilities. The Imperial franchise still remains vested exclusively in the people of the United Kingdom, and upon them exclusively devolve all the responsibilities attaching to the defence of the Empire in time of war, and the maintenance, defence, and advancement of the rights and interests of individual British subjects, of the several countries in the Empire, and of the Empire as a whole in time of peace. There are other aspects in which the Imperial relationship may be viewed, but herein lies its fundamental difficulty.

We are now in a position to look into the situation more closely. What is the actual working of the present anomalous arrangement ? To the Colonies it means that, while on the one hand they escape altogether the political difficulty, the labour and expense, the money-tax and the blood-tax, involved in responsibility for the maintenance and defence of the Empire in all its foreign relations, they find themselves, on the other hand, without any constitutional voice in foreign affairs —even when these nearly affect their own special interests—and are unable to carry out or procure the adoption by the mother-country of any foreign policy, however much they may desire it. Witness the annexation of New Guinea, attempted, on behalf of Australia, by the colony of Queensland, but vetoed by the Government of the United Kingdom, and the whole annexation policy of Australia in the South Pacific continually pressed upon the Home Government, and that Government's steady refusal to carry it out. They find themselves at the same time exposed to the inconvenience and risks of wars entered upon by the Government of the United Kingdom—wars in which it is possible they may—some of them at any rate—have no direct interest, and in the making or ending of which they have no part or voice.

How does this affect the United Kingdom? In the first place, the people of the United Kingdom have to bear the whole pecuniary expense of the four services concerned with foreign affairs (with the exception of some military contributions from India and the Crown Colonies), the advantages of which are shared by all parts of the Empire and every individual in it alike. And, more than that, they may be called upon to undertake a war, involving untold loss and misery and enormous expense to themselves on account of some single one of the Colonies. On whatever account the war, the whole Empire suffers in some way, or at least, runs the risk of suffering, but in all cases the United Kingdom immeasurably the most of all. Colonists, referring to these risks, sometimes talk of Great Britain going to war in some cause that does not concern them. There might be a war in which not all the Colonies would have a direct interest, as, for instance, if we went to war with France on behalf of Newfoundland, or with America on behalf of Canadian interests in Bering Sea or elsewhere. Australasia and South Africa would have no direct interest there, but neither would the United Kingdom itself. Historically, the facts are all the other way. Britain's quarrels for the last three centuries, wherever the theatre of war may have been, and whatever the ostensible *casus belli*, have not been fought on grounds concerning Britain herself, but have been in one way or another Colonial wars ; and Britain's only danger of war now lies, not at home, but in one corner or the other of the outlying Empire. A war with Russia, even, would not in the future any more than in the past arise from any danger threatening these Islands, but from the danger that threatens our lines of communication and those of the Colonies, that threatens India, and, more remotely, Australasia in the South, and Canada in the North, Pacific.

The existing anomalous condition of the Imperial relationship has grown up, as we have seen, from the partial nature of the transition from the absolute dependence of the Colonies to the position they now enjoy. So long as they were in a completely dependent position, and the territories themselves remained the property of the people of Great Britain and Ireland, it was only right and natural that the mother-country should mainly undertake the work of Imperial defence as well as the control also of local defences. When the Colonies obtained domestic self-government and the

ownership of their own lands they were left to supply
their own local defences, for which this country then
ceased to be responsible, but were not then wealthy
enough to undertake the expense, or politically advanced
enough to be intrusted with the responsibility, of sharing in any Imperial obligations, whether of defence or
otherwise. But their growth has been, and continues
to be, very rapid; and things have reached a stage
now, when on both sides it is felt that the present
loose and anomalous relationship is unsatisfactory, for
different reasons, to both parties to it, and fraught with
danger to the maintenance of Imperial unity. The
anomalous nature to-day of a state of things that was
all very well even a generation ago becomes trans-
parently plain when we compare the material condition
of the Colonies then and now.

In a paper which I read in 1886, before the Royal
United Service Institution, upon " Imperial Federation :
Naval and Military," some of the most striking comparisons were brought out between the material development of the Empire at the period of the great Exhibition of 1851, and at that of the Colonial and Indian
Exhibition of 1886. These were illustrated by diagrams ;
and it is not a little significant that many items in the
comparison, in which the Colonial portion bulks large
in 1886, were in 1851 too small to admit of illustration
on the scale adopted. The Consolidation of the British
Empire is, I understand, to form the subject of a
special paper in this series ; but, without trenching
unduly on the province of that paper, it will be useful,
in this preliminary exposition of the case for consideration, to notice some of the main outlines in the picture
of the Empire drawn in the lecture referred to, and

some further statements made by myself, in the House of Commons, in dealing only a few months ago with the question of the growth of Colonial sea-borne commerce and the need of naval defence.

In 1851 the trade of the Colonies (which throughout must be taken to mean British North America, Australasia, and South Africa, as distinguished from Dependencies like India, Ceylon, West Indies, &c.) amounted to 24 millions of pounds sterling. In 1884–85 the same trade had risen to 176 millions. A similar comparison for the whole Empire between the two Exhibition years, 1851 and 1886, brings out the fact of the following astounding growth. In 1851 the total trade of the Empire, United Kingdom, Colonies, and Dependencies, added together, amounted to not quite 400 millions (£399,765,796), of which that of the United Kingdom counted for 324 millions, odd. In 1886 the total stood at 1079 millions odd, of which the United Kingdom supplied 644 millions, the Dependencies 258 millions, and the Colonies the balance of 176 millions.

Between the same periods, 1851 and 1886, the growth in shipping annually entered and cleared at British ports was equally remarkable. At the former date the movements of shipping in the Colonies, being less than 5 million tons, could not be illustrated in the diagrams on the scale necessarily adopted to bring the measurements for the whole Empire within manageable limits. It was then only 4 millions and three-quarters tons, while in 1884–85 it had risen to 26 millions and a half. The totals of such movements of shipping for the Empire, for 1851, gave a little over 25 millions and a quarter tons (25,283,241), of which the United Kingdom had 14 millions and a half. In 1886 the total stood at

141 million tons. And here, it is to be noticed, the proportions have to be reversed. The share of the United Kingdom is 64 millions against 67 millions provided by the Dependencies (51 millions) and the Colonies (16 millions).

The bearing of these figures on the question of Imperial Defence, which means primarily the defence of sea-borne commerce, is, of course, obvious; and, in the same paper, two other comparisons were made, giving direct point to this connection. One of these compared, on the one side, the trade of the five principal countries (exclusive of the United States) having sea-boards on the Pacific Ocean, and, on the other, their effective naval power. The countries were Peru, Japan, Chili, China, and Australasia, in the order of an ascending scale of their commerce. The trade of Peru and Japan was comparatively insignificant; that of Chili about a quarter, and of China less than half, of Australasia. On the other side, we find that Peru's navy had recently been destroyed in the war with Chili; Japan at that date maintained 7 sea-going modern cruisers, Chili 8, and China 7, irrespective in all cases of ships of other classes. What do we find against Australasia, whose trade exceeds that of all the others put together? The entry at the time was, "Australasia maintains no ocean cruisers."

The other table compared the Colonies (in the same sense as here throughout) with the United States of America—a country inhabited by an equally industrial and peace-loving population. The area of the Colonies is a little over 7 million square miles; that of the United States a little over 3 millions. The Colonial trade was 176 millions, against 293 millions for the

United States; the revenue 37 millions and a half, against 72 millions and a half. But the " Expenditure on War Forces" by the States was 11 millions and three-quarters, while that of the Colonies was "incapable of being shown on the diagram," being but little more than the odd three-quarters of a million (£802,559).

On the motion for going into Committee of Supply on the Navy Estimates in March last, I raised a debate by "calling attention" to the growth of Colonial maritime commerce, and the increase of British naval responsibilities caused thereby. I pointed out that our Home population was now dependent on maritime trade for food, and, I might have added, for the means of buying it to be gained by working up the raw materials, the supply of which also depends on the safety of our ocean-trade. Formerly, danger to our commerce was virtually confined to European waters and the North-West Atlantic. The area of danger now includes every sea in the World. At the close of our great European war (1815), the commerce to be protected was that of the United Kingdom alone. At that time, though we had already asserted the supremacy of the seas, and had only the germs of an outlying empire to defend, the naval estimates were £22,000,000. For the present year the estimate is only something over £14,000,000; and we have to protect an immense empire, having a vastly extended area and an enormously increased sea-commerce.

The increase over, roughly, fifty years—from the commencement of Her Majesty's reign—is shown by the following figures. In 1837 the annual revenue of the United Kingdom was 55 millions, and the

annual sea-commerce was valued at 155 millions. At
the present day the revenue is 89 millions, and the sea-
commerce 744 millions. But a much larger proportionate growth of sea-commerce is shown on the side of the
outlying portions of the Empire. The aggregate revenue
of these was, at the beginning of the reign, 23 millions,
against 105 millions now ; while the sea-commerce,
then under 55 millions, has now risen to 460 millions.
During this period, therefore, the revenue of the
United Kingdom has increased only by about one-
half, and the sea-commerce has increased five times,
while the revenue of the rest of the Empire has increased nearly five times, and its sea-commerce about
nine times. Of 194 millions of revenue raised last year
throughout the Empire, 105 millions were raised in the
outlying parts; and that portion constantly increases,
whilst that of the United Kingdom remains about
stationary.

Here, then, we have a very pregnant comparison
indeed. But there is more behind. The commerce of
the outlying portions of the Empire is capable of
division into two classes—that carried on with the
United Kingdom, in which, therefore, the United
Kingdom is equally interested, and that carried on in-
dependently. The former is put down at 187 millions,
the latter at 273 millions, per annum. It is accordingly not only the trade of the rest of the Empire
rather than that of the United Kingdom which has
so greatly increased the bulk of the commerce requiring naval protection, but it is in chief part their independent trade in which the United Kingdom has no
direct interest whatever. This independent sea-borne
trade of the outlying portions of the Empire is four

times that of Russia, two and a half times that of Italy, about half that of the United States, nearly equal to that of Germany, and about three-quarters that of France; and it is increasing every year at such a rate as to be fast overtaking the sea-borne commerce of the United Kingdom itself.

And how is the naval protection of this commerce— the commerce of the whole British Empire, of which so large a proportion is of the character shown—how is its protection provided and paid for? Let it be borne in mind that the commerce of the United Kingdom requiring protection is valued at 744 millions; that of the rest of the Empire 460 millions, of which 273 millions have no connection with the United Kingdom at all. Well, the United Kingdom finds 14 millions and a quarter of the cost, the rest of the Empire 381 *thousands*. Of this not very magnificent total India alone finds 254 thousands (two-thirds of which, however, is for troopships and harbours, not for sea-going vessels protecting trade), and the balance, except some few hundreds, consists of the £126,000 to be contributed by Australasia towards the cost of the local squadron to cruise in its own waters exclusively.

Out of every pound sterling spent during the current year for the naval protection of the Empire the outlying portions will spend about 6¼d., and the United Kingdom the balance of 19s. 5¾d.

Enough of these comparisons, taken from the sources already indicated, have been given to demonstrate very clearly two or three propositions. First, the provision made for Imperial Defence is very far indeed from keeping pace with Imperial property requiring defence. Second, the growth of commerce, which causes the increase of property to be defended, is much more rapid in the outlying Empire than in the United Kingdom; and of that growing commerce outside the United Kingdom the major part is independent, and has no direct interest whatever for the United Kingdom. Third, the United Kingdom bears practically the entire burden of the defence of the commerce of the whole Empire, to which India contributes an insignificant quota, and the self-governing Colonies simply nothing at all—for the other small quota from Australasia figuring in the Estimates is devoted to local, not Imperial, defence, and is demonstrably no relief whatever to the expenditure of the United Kingdom, which was increased *pari passu* with that contribution.

If we turn for a moment from the navy to the army, we find that towards the expense of this arm of defence the self-governing Colonies contribute nothing at all, while the Dependencies do. Looking at the Diplomatic Service, we see at this moment the whole burden of Canada's dispute with the United States being borne by the British Foreign Office and its Diplomatic agents, while the Canadian Government merely look on and criticise, and they and the whole people of Canada are able to devote themselves to fighting a general election in which this grave question plays no part whatever. We see also, at this very moment, the Foreign Office and the Colonial Office engaged in most difficult negotiations with France on behalf of Newfoundland in her dispute with that Power; while, again, the Government and people of Newfoundland not only lend no help—not only even stand by and criticise—but, in addition to criticising, refuse to move a finger to help their champion. Apart from the Diplomatic Service proper there is the Consular establishment of Great Britain in every country on the face of the globe, by means of which every business man in the Colonies is being assisted, either directly or indirectly, year in and year out. In short, every individual Colonist gets the full advantage of being a citizen of one of the oldest, richest, and most powerful States in the World without either, directly or indirectly, paying one penny-piece for the privilege.

Such a condition of affairs has not in it the elements of permanency. It is possible, on the one hand, that when the true state of the case comes to be widely known and appreciated in the United Kingdom, the tax-payers may become restive under such an apparently one-sided bargain. On the other hand, the Colonies, though well enough satisfied at present with an arrangement that relieves them of expense and responsibility, may not always be content, even at a saving to their pockets, to have their foreign relations managed for them as they now are. Moreover, there is room for very grave doubt as to whether the protection of the mother-country would prove, in the actual event of war, as effective as is assumed. In addition to the probability of the fleet proving inadequate to the large responsibilities to be faced, it is pretty certain that, in the event of the food-supplies of the United Kingdom being seriously threatened, the British tax-payer would insist on the whole strength of his navy being concentrated for their protection. At present, however, the Colonists do not seem to concern themselves about this.

There are two directions in which men's thoughts are moving in the Colonies in connection with this question. Among some there is a tendency to consider the complications and risk of being dragged into war entailed by the Imperial connection too high a price to pay for the gratuitous support and protection afforded by the mother-country. Another and more high-spirited feeling is also working against the continuance of the existing relations. Men in the Colonies, who have minds above greed alone, and can speak their minds without having the fear of ignorant constituents before their eyes, feel the irksomeness and humiliation of their present position. They cannot tolerate that their otherwise free countries should continue, *vis-à-vis* of the outside World, to be in the position of mere dependents, living under the protection of a wealthy patron. Such men desire, accordingly, either to come forward and take up the full citizenship of the Empire, or to sever the connection altogether, and stand boldly before the World in their own right and by their own strength. Many men, and not a few of considerable political eminence, have spoken openly of separation, as we all know—unless, as perhaps we ought, we except Lord Carrington, whose high office in New South Wales appears to have prevented his knowing what was notorious to every one else, and was openly canvassed in the press and in Parliament. Now, however much the idea of separation is to be deprecated by patriotic Britons in all parts of the World, it has to be remembered that the time is past for disputing the right of the great groups to sever their political connection with the mother-country, if in their wisdom, or unwisdom, they should definitely and solemnly elect to do so. The whole case to the contrary was given away when the Colonies were granted responsible government, and with it the absolute ownership of their land, freed from its share in the public debt, and the complete control of their finances and tariffs without any reservation of any sort or kind calculated to maintain the political union inviolate. In fact, the policy which found public expression in the speeches of the apostles of the old Manchester School determined the policy of British government in those days. The Colonies were repeatedly told they were free to go, not without a hint that the sooner they availed themselves of that freedom the better. Responsible government was conceded as a stepping-stone to independence, which was officially regarded as their natural destiny.

Now, however, a large numerical majority of the people on both sides the sea, and almost all the leaders of opinion and far-seeing and responsible members of the community throughout the Empire, recognise that separation would be a mistake. But there is, in consequence of the fatal errors of policy committed by a former generation of British statesmen and publicists, an alarming amount of leeway to be made up. The question of the maintenance of the Imperial connection anywhere is an open one; and it is this uncertainty as to the future that paralyses community of action. If it be practically an open question whether or not the Colonies will one by one cut themselves adrift, as and whenever it suits their individual convenience to do so, it is the height of folly for the United Kingdom to continue to do everything for them, and treat them in all respects in a manner only reasonably compatible with a sense of their permanent union with itself. On the other hand, the Colonies naturally desire to pro-

long the present happy state of things; while in some
cases, perhaps, they would in any circumstance hesitate
to take an irretrievable step in the direction of a closer
union on a permanent footing, not having quite made
up their minds what they would best like to do ulti-
mately, when the present halcyon days come to an end
for them.

Until the question is fairly faced—as it will have to
be faced before very long—no great progress can be
made.   It behoves both sides, therefore, to consider
what the effect of separation would be.   Without going
over the whole ground, it is easy to show, upon the one
case of naval and military defence, that the interests of
both the mother-country and the Colonies alike are
bound up in the maintenance of political unity.   Both
alike are equally interested in keeping open and protecting from interference the great trade-routes of the
World in time of war as well as in peace.   As it has
been well put, "Above all questions of Free Trade or of
fair trade is the paramount question of safe trade."

To the United Kingdom the safety of its food-supplies
and the routes for what is a necessity second only to the
supply of food—the supply of the raw materials that
support its mills—is of absolutely vital moment; and it
is the possession of naval bases in every sea that largely
contributes to this safety.   If Australia, for example,
were independent, and an alien though friendly nation,
her ports, dockyards, and coaling-stations would be open
to the ships of Her Majesty's navy when engaged in
war, only on precisely the same terms as to those of the
enemy.   While, if Australia were at war with another
Power,—France, for instance,—Britain being neutral—
this country would be powerless, while maintaining her

neutrality, to prevent the blockade of Australian ports, whereby our supplies of wool would be cut off from that quarter. The case, in fact, might reproduce the results that followed in our centres of industry from the blockade of the cotton-ports in the American civil war.

Again, if for Australia we instance Canada, the same results would follow, with the difference that for " wool " we must now read " food." Canada is more and more becoming, and likely to become, the granary of the United Kingdom, so that our food-supplies from that source increase in importance every year. Or, to complete the circle, let us suppose South Africa independent. We are at war, and South Africa is neutral. Result: our enemy's fleet can do that which it cannot do now— coal at the Cape, and steam on to the attack of India or Australia.

To the Colonies, the first and most palpable result of separation would be felt on the financial side. They depend for their development on the public and private loans obtained in such abundance from England; and the golden stream, if it did not dry up, would promptly cease to flow so smoothly, on such easy terms, to countries no longer under the British flag. " Cheap money " is to these young communities as the breath of their nostrils. They are deeply anxious now to obtain the right of having their public stocks placed on the list of investments sanctioned for trust funds, in order to raise the price of their stocks, and so enable them to obtain money still more cheaply. Obviously, the effect of separation would be to lower these stocks and their credit, public and private, very materially; and this is a contingency their politicians and public men have no desire to face.

Just at the time when facilities for borrowing were thus seriously checked, they would at once have to set to work and undertake expenses beyond any they have ever dreamt of to provide for their security against foreign aggression. They would have to set up a complete naval equipment—ships, guns, dockyards, arsenals, an Admiralty Department, and a force of officers and seamen; some would have to materially increase their military forces, horse, foot, and artillery; and they would have to set up a Foreign Office, with a staff of Diplomatic representatives and Consular officers in all the civilised and half-civilised countries with which they have any dealings, political or commercial.

Much of this seems scarcely to have suggested itself to the run of politicians and writers in the Colonies. They have thought something of the question of defending their shores from foreign enemies, but have for the most part altogether failed to get a real grasp of what that means. They think that, as they already provide for the land-defence of their own coasts, the only addition they would have to make would be at most the establishment of a naval squadron of their own for their own waters, to replace the ships of the Imperial navy now stationed there. This is a very superficial view indeed. The cardinal fact of Imperial Defence is that the safety of each part depends upon the aggregate strength of the whole force of the Empire. It is not alone the few ships on the Australian station (to keep to the same country for illustration) that render Australia safe from attack. It is also the ships in European waters, in North Pacific waters, and elsewhere throughout the World, which, by closing up the hostile ports of issue at the commencement of a war, would prevent the despatch of an expedition in force too great to be resisted by the squadron of local defence. Moreover, it is not the fear of that squadron or of Australia's land-defences that would make a foreign Power hesitate on occasion to attack her, but the knowledge that the whole power of the British Empire is behind her.

The effect of this is found in peace as well as in war. Suppose Australia independent, and having her representatives in the capitals of Europe, with what sort of voice could they speak? What force lying behind them would give a sanction to their remonstrances or their threats? For passive defence, but little; for effective action in the offensive operations of defence, none at all. No; it is the power to back a word with a blow that gives effectiveness to words; or, where the case does not go to such lengths, it is the authority and prestige of a great, powerful, and historic nation, having a place among the Powers of the World, that cause the voice of its ambassadors to be listened to with respect, and their words to carry weight and influence. Of all this, in peace and war, the Colonies have now the incalculable advantage, though they scarcely recognise it. They would find out the difference all too soon and too surely if they threw away their birthright, and found themselves ranking in the World with the groups of republics in South America.

And if the power of the United Kingdom, strengthened at present only by the vague and shadowy reserve of unapplied force, afforded by her outlying Colonies and Dependencies, is so great as it is now, what would not the might of the Empire become if all its scattered resources were welded into one homogeneous whole? Under a complete federation for defence with an

Imperial navy, and each part doing its share of land-defence and co-operating with the navy, in pursuance of an ordered and uniform system, the effective power of the Empire for defence would be multiplied in a ratio out of all proportion to the mere sum of the forces of its several parts.   It would be able to defy attack, and would form a League of Peace capable of enforcing its will—so long as its will meant peace—upon the World.

But though federation, as regards matters of actual relations, and especially for defence, is at once the most important and the most pressing part of the Federal problem, it is not quite the whole of it.   There are other lines along which the movement might travel, many matters calling for joint action, all helping towards the attainment of national unity.   The exigencies of space forbid more than a bare mention of these elements of unity, but their mere mention will be sufficiently suggestive.   Under the head of "Communications" much could be written.   Some steps have been taken by the governments of the United Kingdom, and both of the Colonies and Dependencies towards common action in Postal matters, that may lead, it is hoped, to far more uniformity than at present exists in this respect.   Here, and in another branch of communications—Telegraphs—the goal to be aimed at is the recognition of the Empire as a solid unit.   Every step in this direction is a step towards political federation which must make itself useful in other branches of administration as well.

Law is a thorny subject; but it is one in which an enormous amount of advantage would be gained by more concerted action between the various parts of the

Empire.   The principle of this is already recognised by the passage of statutes having the effect of extending the legal processes of each part of the Empire to other parts, and generally providing for the recognition throughout the Empire of legal rights and obligations, in whatever part of it originating.   The discussions of the Imperial Conference of 1887, and of the conferences held among themselves by the Colonies of the Australasian group, show how great need exists for concerted action in this direction; and few things would exercise a more practically binding effect than the extended recognition of the unity of the Empire by further advances along this line.   Business men as well as lawyers will see at once the work that has to be done here in bankruptcy and commercial law, and the execution of process in these branches and in criminal cases, copyright. trademarks, &c.

The status of the Home and Colonial Civil Services and of the learned professions and others, and the reciprocal recognition throughout the Empire of these ranks and diplomas, would also lend themselves to similar treatment.   Emigration and colonisation are now subjects of great difficulty.   The replies sent in by the Colonial Governments to the questions submitted to them, the report of the Colonisation Committee, which has just been issued, and the evidence of Agents-General and other witnesses, all show that, as things stand, the attitude of the Colonies renders impossible any attempt by the Home Government to plant our surplus population on the vast tracts of land lying unoccupied in the Colonies.

The question of tariffs attracts much attention just at present; and some persons see in it the means by which Britannic Confederation can best be achieved. It is one of the subjects to be specially treated in a separate paper. It will be sufficient here to point out that, however desirable it may be to promote the intercourse of trade within the Empire, there are at present formidable obstacles in the way of attempts to do this, whichever direction such attempts take. If it be sought to establish an Imperial *Zollverein* with Free Trade within the Empire, there is the obstacle of the Colonial tariffs, which are almost universally protective; and the Colonists show no disposition to relax these tariffs, which, apart from protecting their young industries against the competition of the cheaper production of the mother-country, are by all of them presently regarded as necessarily the chief source of revenue in countries too young in the accumulation of wealth to stand heavy direct taxation. If, on the other hand, it be proposed to keep up in the Colonies a tariff-wall against the goods of the United Kingdom, only raising it somewhat higher against outsiders, this, on the one hand, would not benefit the United Kingdom, while, on the other hand, it would involve the imposition of import duties against foreign countries by the United Kingdom; and these, to be of any use by way of giving a preference to the Colonies, must be on their chief productions, food-stuffs, and the raw material of manufactures, to increase the cost of which is a course that does not at present, in the absence of any substantial countervailing advantage, commend itself to the people of this country. Community of trade interests would undoubtedly be most valuable in cementing the bonds of national unity. But there are lines of less resistance along which the movement to that end can just now more safely proceed.

Before concluding this, perhaps, too lengthy paper, it seems fitting to make some reference to the work of the Imperial Federation League, to which is due in so large a measure the position which the Colonial Question now occupies in the politics of the day, and the great change that has come over the public mind upon the future of the Imperial relationship within the past few years. Formed in 1884, at a Conference held in London, and presided over by the Right Hon. W. E. Forster, this League has now assumed almost the proportions of a national, or—though the two words ought really to mean the same thing when applied as they are here — Imperial, organisation. The Conference laid down in its resolutions three fundamental propositions, which are as follows :—(1) That, in order to secure the permanent unity of the Empire some form of Federation is essential ; (2) that no scheme of Federation should interfere with the existing rights of local parliaments as regards local affairs ; and (3) that any scheme of Imperial Federation should combine on an equitable basis the resources of the Empire for the maintenance of common interests, and adequately provide for an organised defence of common rights. These are broad and statesmanlike propositions, and they have withstood the fire of criticism—and the League has been subject to a pretty constant, if not always very heavy, fire— during the seven years that have passed since they were adopted as the constitution and charter of the League.

The principal aim of the League hitherto has been to diffuse information and form public opinion on the subject of the Colonial Question both at home and in the Colonies. The measure of its attainment of these ends may be gauged by any one who will merely glance over files of newspapers and reviews for 1883 and 1884, and then for 1889–1890. To the action of the League, moreover, was directly due the convocation of the Imperial Conference of 1887, which, besides making a small beginning on the principle of common action in naval defence, though not quite on federal lines, was the means of showing how much required to be done in the way of common action, and how it might be done by discussions and action by Federal Councils at conferences.

In conclusion, it may, perhaps, be well to say that in this paper Federation for Defence has been given so outstanding a prominence for two reasons. First, it would have deserved and required such prominence in any case, because, in the opinion of the writer, it constitutes eight-tenths of the whole question of Federation. Secondly, it seemed to call for such treatment, especially in this introductory paper, because, though other branches of the subject are set down for separate treatment, no specific mention of "Defence" is made at all in the syllabus of papers to follow this one, and it would therefore have to be treated, it is presumed, under the general head of "Political." This seemed a sufficient reason for dwelling at length upon it here even to the partial exclusion of other topics.

In closing this article I must express my indebtedness to Mr. Robert Beadon—a member of the Executive Committee of the Imperial Federation League—without whose aid it could not, owing to other demands upon my attention, have been prepared in time for publication.

J. COLOMB.

II.

THE PHYSICAL AND POLITICAL BASES OF NATIONAL UNITY.

By EDWARD A. FREEMAN, M.A., D.C.L., LL.D.,

Regius Professor of Modern History at the University of Oxford.

THE PHYSICAL AND POLITICAL BASES OF NATIONAL UNITY.

I FEEL it a great honour to be asked to write a paper in a series to the seeming object of which I am altogether opposed. Such a request shows a willingness to listen to what is to be said on the other side, which is not common in modern controversy. It is a feeling which I thoroughly return. There is no living writer whom I read more gladly and with more profit that Mr. Dicey. I am a Home-Ruler; he is an Unionist. But I know that in his writings I shall always find the case for the other side as clearly and powerfully put as it can be. And that is a great help towards being able to put the case for one's own side clearly and powerfully. There would be fewer controversies in the World than there are, and those that could not be avoided would be carried on more reasonably than they are, if only each side thoroughly understood what the other side means, and further, what is sometimes harder still, if each side thoroughly understood what it means itself.

The heading of this article is one given to me, not one of my own choice. Considering the purpose of the series, the main practical object of discussion which it suggests would seem to be whether the actual conditions of the World, and specially its geographical conditions, will allow the existence of national unity, or such measure of it as may be implied in the word "Confederation," between certain communities scattered over very distant parts of the World. In discussing this question, as in discussing any other question, it is needful first of all to know what it is that we are discussing. That is, we must fully make up our minds as to the meaning in which we intend to use the chief words which we use in the discussion. In this discussion let us see, first of all, what we mean by National Unity.

I have gone very fully in another place into the question as to what constitutes a nation ; * what I have said there I must often assume now. The word *Nation* is constantly used in very different senses, and much confusion arises from its use in different senses. In some cases it is simply used as equivalent to *independent power*. It is used thus when we speak of *international* relations, when we ask, purely for purposes of international law, of what *nationality* a man is. In answering such a question as this, the Swiss Confederation and the Austro-Hungarian Monarchy each passes for a nation. The several Spanish-speaking commonwealths of North and South America pass for distinct nations. A Greek of the kingdom of Greece and a Greek who is a subject of the Turkish Sultan pass for men of different nationalities. So do an Italian-speaking man at Trent, another at Verona, and a third at Lugano. But this use of the word *nation* and its derivatives is confined to the formal range of international politics. As soon as we get beyond that formal range, as soon as we pass

---

* I refer, as I often have to do, to the Essay on "Race and Language," which first appeared in the *Contemporary Review* for March 1877, and which is reprinted in my "Third Series of Historical Essays," p. 173.

from what is to what has been, to what may be, or to
what ought to be, our use of the word *nation* begins to
be affected by other considerations. To prove that men
belong to the same nation, it is no longer quite enough
to show that they are subjects or citizens of the same
political power. To prove that they belong to different nations, it is no longer enough to show that they
are subjects or citizens of different powers. A man's
nationality becomes rather a good deal wider than the
simple question to what minister or consul he must apply
if he needs help in a foreign country. As soon as we
begin to think of nationality in this wider sense, we feel
that, besides the distinction of political powers, there is
something else to be thought of which is not so easy to
define. The thought of community of blood, of community of language, of fellowship in the events of past
times, all come in. And yet we presently begin to feel
that we cannot build up a theory of " National Unity "
on any one of these things by itself. So to do would
soon lead us as far astray as we should be led by the
formal doctrine of international law. We gradually
come to see that there is such a thing as an idea of a
nation in the mind, but that such an idea hardly ever
answers to anything that has any actual being on earth.
Does it at all follow that the idea of a nation that we
have in the mind is a mere dream, unpractical folly, and
the like? A mere dream it certainly is in one sense;
unpractical folly it certainly is not. The ideal notion
of a nation is like any other counsel of perfection. Such
a counsel is a model to which every man cannot attain,
to which very likely no man can attain, but which every
man is the better for keeping before him and getting as
near to it as he can. It may therefore be worth while

to try to give an ideal definition of a nation, even
though it may be very hard, perhaps quite impossible,
to find any existing nation which answers to it.

The ideal nation then, I would say, is to be found
where a continuous territory is inhabited by a people
united under one government, and all of them speaking
the same language, a language which is not spoken by
any other people.

It will be noticed that I am satisfied with unity of
language, and that I say nothing about unity of race.
The question of race is too deep for our present inquiry.
It doubtless is a practical question. That is, there is
every reason to think that strict community of blood,*
where it exists, has a real influence. But that influence
works in such silent and uncertain ways that we cannot
reckon on it as an element in our calculations. We
must take the outward sign of language instead of it.
Community of language is doubtless often a witness
to real community of blood; it is very often only its
substitute. We know that it is so in many cases; we
suspect that it may be so in many others. But in
practical matters it is the only test that we can go by.
And we must take the word *language* in its rough
practical sense. It does not shut out wide differences
of dialect. It is enough if the speakers of each dialect
understand the speakers of every other. Indeed I should
rather say that it was enough if there is one central
dialect which is understood by the speakers of all the

* When I speak of "community of blood," I do so under the
limitations drawn in the article above quoted. It is always possible
that, even where there is community of *race*, in the strictest sense
of the word *race* to which we can reach, there may be no physical
community of blood.

others. In the sense with which we are concerned, all Great Britain and Ireland speaks English, except so much as speaks Welsh, Gaelic, or Irish. French and Provençal are historically as truly distinct languages as French and Italian; but, for our purposes, all France speaks French, except so much as speaks Basque, Breton, or Flemish.

Now, taking this definition of an ideal nation, it might be rash to say that there is nothing answering to it in any part of the World. But it is quite certain that there is nothing exactly answering to it among the civilised States of Europe and America. It is equally certain that some of those States come much nearer to the model than others. Among those which rank as "Great Powers" the kingdom of Italy may from one side be said to reach it. The dialects of Italian are many and strongly marked; but, as language has been defined above, we may fairly say that the whole kingdom speaks Italian.* And on the other side, though there is an *Italia Irredenta*, it is small compared with the large districts out of the German Empire which speak German. France, as far as Europe is concerned, comes on one side nearer to the model than Italy. There is a lost territory which France wishes to win back, but it can hardly be called a *Francia Irredenta*. Germany is further off from the model on both sides; Russia is on one side

---

* I do not forget that within the kingdom of Italy there is a district that speaks French (or Provençal), another that speaks German, and another that speaks Slav. But they are districts which are almost invisible, and which may be said to come under the rule, "*De minimis non curat lex.*" The non-French-speaking parts of France are much greater, and the non-English-speaking parts of the United Kingdom much greater again.

nearer to it than Italy, for there are few speakers of
Russian out of the Russian Empire; * on the other side
it is much further off than Germany, as the Russian
Empire contains millions on millions who are not
speakers of Russian. Still, Russia and Germany are
both national powers; if they contain non-Russian and
non-German elements, it is the Russian and German
kernel round which they are gathered which determines
everything. The Austro-Hungarian monarchy stands
among the six Great Powers at the other end. As a
whole, it has no national life or national tie whatever.
Yet, one of its chief members, the kingdom of Hungary,
has both in a large measure. Among the smaller powers
of Europe the same differences may be seen, though
most of them come much nearer to national unity than
the great ones. Switzerland stands out among them
all, a power made up by the union of fragments of other
powers, speaking four languages within its borders,†
and yet possessed of a true national life. Its example
shows that, as language habitually takes the place of
race in the formation of nations, so, under special circumstances, political necessities can take the place of
language.

Of the six Great Powers, as they usually are called, I

---

* Only the Ruthenians, the Russians of Red Russia, in the kingdom of Galicia and Lodomeria, one of the possessions of the House
of Austria.

† German, French, and Italian are acknowledged by the Confederation as national languages. The fourth speech, the Romansch
of Graubünden, is not. This is most likely because the other three,
as the languages of Great Powers outside the Confederation, proclaim themselves as independent languages, while Romansch has
the look of a mere dialect. But it is the independent speech of
part of Switzerland, and it is not a dialect of any of the other three.

have mentioned five. One remains, that with which we are ourselves most nearly concerned. The power of Great Britain has a very different air, according as we look at it simply as an European power or as a power spreading into all parts of the World. In the former character it comes on one side nearer to the definition of the model nation than any of the other Great Powers. If English is by no means the exclusive language of the United Kingdom, yet the United Kingdom takes in all that part of Europe where English is a natural language; the United Kingdom and its Dependencies take in all that part of Europe where English is spoken at all.* And I have kept back till now one point of the original definition, namely, that the territory of the ideal nation should be *continuous.* Of course this definition is not meant to cut out every case where a territory may consist either of a group of islands or of a piece of mainland with islands lying near to it. Greece and Denmark are obvious instances. Italy might cause a moment's thought; Capri, Elba, Sicily, and Sardinia might seem to stand in four different relations to the peninsular kingdom; but we need not stop to examine the point, which just now is not a practical one. About France, Germany, Russia, there is not much to say in the way of islands. That Jersey, Guernsey, and their fellows, have been for ages dependencies of England, and have not been incorporated with France, shows how

---

* I have to make this distinction, because Man and the Channel Islands are not part of the United Kingdom, but dependencies of it. And in them, though English has made a certain progress, it is not the natural language. In more distant Dependencies, as Malta, however many people may find it convenient to learn English, it is strictly a foreign language.

geography may sometimes have to yield to manifest
interest and to a historic tie. With this exception, the
islands attached to each of those powers follow naturally
on the possession of the neighbouring coast. If any
one grudges the possession of Åland by Russia, the
other chance is that it should go back to Sweden. The
British Possessions in Europe stand on quite another
footing. The United Kingdom consists of two large
islands and a number of smaller ones. In the middle
of them lies the dependency of Man; at some distance
the dependent Channel Islands; and at one end lie
Orkney and Shetland, of which I am not called on to
speak particularly. But islands like Wight, Anglesey,
Bute, may be reasonably called continuous with the Isle
of Britain itself. The only question lies between the
two great islands, Britain and Ireland. Some have
thought that their geographical position—specially with
a distinct, though dependent, State lying between them—
points to a state of things in which they should have a
certain connection with one another, but a connection
less close than that which binds the several parts of
Britain to one another. On this thorny question I will
not enter here. All that concerns us just now is that
the United Kingdom, as it stands at present, is the
one purely insular power among all the powers of
Europe, great and small. The home territory is insular;
so are all the European Dependencies, except one
peninsular rock. And the home territory, at first sight
at least, hangs well together. If we cannot always walk
from one part to another, it is practically as continuous
as many continental territories. No foreign territory
comes between any part of it and any other part; and
it has one great advantage over all continental terri-

tories, namely, that it has no frontier towards any foreign country.

Having thus got some notion of the conditions of national unity as they exist in Europe, we go on to the further question, what those conditions are, and whether there are any such conditions in the case of lands which are in quite another case from the lands of Europe? Is national unity, in any sense at all approaching to our definition of it, or indeed in any sense, possible in the case of territories which do not lie continuous in Europe or in any other part of the World, but which are scattered over all the regions of the Earth, over distant continents and islands, parted from one another by vast stretches of Ocean? How does the case stand when, to go from one part to another, large foreign territories have sometimes to be crossed, constantly either to be crossed or gone round? That a scattered dominion like this can be held together by allegiance to a common sovereign or to a common ruling city is shown by many examples in various ages. Such was the dominion of Carthage, Athens, Venice, and Genoa, in the Mediterranean, in days when the Mediterranean was what the Ocean is now.* Such has been the dominion of Portugal, Spain, France, Holland, England, since the Ocean has become what the Mediterranean once was. And experience also proves that the central power may either hold a despotic rule over its distant dependencies, or may grant them the highest measure of internal freedom con-

* The unbroken dominion of Rome does not come in here. Though, or rather because, it took in the dominion of all the cities mentioned in the text, it was not scattered but continuous. But in after times the Roman power at Constantinople did become a scattered dominion, like that of Carthage and Venice.

sistent with their remaining dependencies. But here
the line is drawn. At this moment most of the Colonies
of Britain enjoy, in all ordinary times, each one within
its own bounds, very nearly as full an amount of freedom
as if it were an independent State. But in any wider
relations it has no voice. It can have no dealings with
foreign powers ; those it must leave to the central power
which acts on its behalf, as on behalf of all the other
Possessions of the common sovereign. Nay, it cannot
of itself enter into closer relations with its immediate
neighbours. The so-called Confederation of Canada did
not, like the Confederation of the United States, come
into being by the act of its own members. It exists by
virtue of an Act of the Parliament of the United Kingdom. That Act doubtless expresses the wishes of the
lands concerned ; but those lands might have wished for
ever if the British Parliament had not put their wishes
into a practical shape. That is to say, all these lands,
whether remaining as separate colonies or united into
the shape of a Confederation, are simply Dependencies
of the United Kingdom, enjoying such privileges as the
Parliament of the United Kingdom may think good to
grant to them. That supreme power can at any moment
override even internal independence ; it can legislate at
pleasure for the dependency even against its will. Till
quite lately we used to say that, though such a power
existed in theory, it was not likely to be carried out in
practice. But sleeping lions sometimes wake, and we
have just seen the supreme authority of the British
Parliament over a British dependency carried out in its
fulness.

Now suppose the people of the Dependencies—those
Dependencies, I mean, which are practically independent

within their own range—become dissatisfied with their dependent state, and wish, to put the case plainly, to be put on a level with the people of the United Kingdom. That is, suppose they wish, not only to manage their own internal affairs, but to have a voice, in some shape or other, in all affairs that may concern them. It is obvious that there is one way in which this may be had. It may be won in the same way in which it was won by the Thirteen Colonies which became independent in 1776. That is, the act might take the same shape, though the course which led to it might be quite different. That is to say, the mother-country and the colony might part asunder, not through war, like the Thirteen Colonies and the colonies of Spain, but peacefully, as Portugal and Brazil parted asunder. And if any Colony now enjoying internal freedom chose to put forth a Declaration of Independence, it is not likely that the mother-country would constrain it by force to remain in a state of dependence. But, supposing the Dependency wishes that its state of dependence on the mother-country should cease, but that it does not at all wish that its political connection with the mother-country should cease with it. Its people, we may put it, wish to be put on a level with the people of the mother-country, but they do not wish to be put on a level with them by becoming a people wholly apart from the mother-country. They wish to be put on a level with them by being promoted to a voice in certain matters in which the people of the mother-country now have a voice, but in which they have none. But they wish to have a voice in those matters in common with the people of the mother-country, not apart from them.

Now, this is as much as to say that they wish for a

federal union with the mother-country and with one another. There is another form of union, possible in theory, but which is really not worth discussing in practice. I mean that the Colonies might be joined to the United Kingdom in the same way in which Scotland was joined to England and Ireland to Great Britain. Members for the Colonies might be admitted to seats in the Parliament of the United Kingdom. But to carry this plan out consistently would involve the abolition of the separate legislatures of each Colony. One Parliament would legislate for all. By this means the national unity which at present exists between the mother-country and the Colonies would, on its political side, be drawn much closer. All parts of the scattered territory would be politically equal; no part would be dependent on any other part; everything that could be called "national" in any sense would be common to all parts on equal terms. Yet I cannot believe that any Dependency would be willing to purchase closer national unity on such terms as these. Surely every British Colony would refuse to exchange its abiding independent management of its own affairs for a voice in affairs which would concern it only now and then. It had surely better remain dependent than share in an independence which has to be purchased at such a cost. What therefore is really sought for by those who wish for some closer and higher form of national unity than a relation of dependence is not absorption into the United Kingdom, but some kind of federal union with it. Three questions here arise:—What are the lands which are to enter into a federal union? Is it possible to establish any kind of federal union among such distant and scattered members?

If such an union can be established, will it practically lead to any closer form of national unity?

These questions seem to bring us to the edge of the dark abyss of what is called "Imperial Federation." But I am glad to see that in the present discussion a good deal has been done to make it possible to argue matters more reasonably than can be done when " Imperial Federation" has to be debated. On the principle that language was given man to conceal his thoughts, "Imperial Federation" is surely the wisest name ever thought of. On any other principle it is surely the most foolish. For it is absolutely without meaning; it is a contradiction in terms. "Empire" implies the rule of some person or power over some other; "federal" implies the union of certain powers or communities, presumably on equal terms. What is imperial cannot be federal, and what is federal cannot be imperial.* The power which the Sovereign and Parliament of the United Kingdom exercises over the Colonies and other dependencies of the United Kingdom may, if any one chooses, be called an "imperial" power, though the use of the word leads the way to many confusions. But if the power of the mother-

---

* The only case in which the words "Imperial Federation" could have any meaning would be if they were applied to the German Empire. That Empire is federal in form, and its chief bears the title of Emperor. So far it is an imperial federation. As for the title of its chief, I have often had to remark that the head of a confederation which has kings among its members can hardly be called anything but Emperor. But the position of the Emperor and of the State of which he is the head quite cuts off the German Empire from being reckoned as a real federation. If anything, it is rather a federal empire, an empire in the shape of a federation.

country over the Dependencies is exchanged for a federal union with them, "empire" passes away, and the word "imperial" is out of place. The "empire," if that is to be the word, may be changed into a confederation ; the "imperial" relation of Great Britain towards Australia or Canada may be changed into a federal relation. But a thing cannot be at once "imperial" and federal ; "empire" shuts out confederation, and confederation shuts out "empire." But granted that there is to be a federation of something, what are the members which are to enter into the federal relation to one another? When I have asked this question, I have sometimes been told that Imperial Federation means a confederation of all the Queen's dominions ; sometimes that it means a confederation of all "the English-speaking people." Each of these answers has a meaning ; but they have two very different meanings. Which are we to choose? The English-speaking people and the Queen's dominions are very far from being the same thing. The majority of the Queen's subjects are not English-speaking, and I fancy that the majority of the English-speaking people are not the Queen's subjects.*   A confederation

---

* It is as well not to be positive, and I am writing without figures. But I should fancy that the population of the United States, even if we take off something for European immigrants who have not yet learned English, is greater than that of the United Kingdom and its English-speaking Dependencies. We need not take off anything for the Negroes ; they are certainly not English, but they are English-speaking ; and it is to be supposed that those who asked for a confederation of the English-speaking people meant to include them. In any case, the population of the United States, if not a majority, must be a minority so great as for our purpose to be the same.

of the Queen's dominions, especially if it be called
"imperial," cannot shut out the "Empire" of India;
and if that be let in, the European, white, Christian
—however we choose to distinguish them—part of Her
Majesty's subjects will be a small minority in the
confederation. Great Britain, Canada, Australia, will
always be out-voted by the greater mass of their Asiatic,
dark-skinned, Hindu, Parsee, and Mohammedan fellow-
subjects. And the place of meeting for such a confederation cannot be Westminster or Ottawa or Melbourne;
it must be Delhi, or anywhere that the Asiatic majority may think good. Is this what anybody in Great
Britain, or in any English-speaking colony, wishes
for? I trow not. But "Imperial Federation," defined as a federation of the Queen's dominions, either
means this or it means nothing.

If, on the other hand, Imperial Federation is defined
to mean, as I have seen it defined to mean, a federation
of "the English-speaking people," then it must leave
out the greater part of the Queen's dominions, 'and it
must take in a great deal that lies outside the Queen's
dominions. It must leave out India; it must take in
the United States. And here comes the very pertinent
question, whether the United States would be inclined
either to enter into any confederation of ours or to let
us into their already existing confederation? One thing
is quite certain; the United States will have nothing
to say to any "Imperial Federation": that is—to try
to get a meaning out of a formula which is meaning-
less—to any federation in which some member, like
Thebes or Prussia, exercises a supremacy over the
others which may, if any one chooses, be called "imperial."

These are the only two attempts at defining "Imperial Federation" which I have ever seen. Commonly, when a man talks about "Imperial Federation" he means something else, something very ill-defined, something which, if one better got to understand it, might prove to be wise or foolish, possible or impossible, but which is in no case federation. Sometimes it is something about the post-office, sometimes something about customs and tariffs. These things are all very important; but they are not federation. A *Postverein*, a *Zollverein* — I must be allowed to use the native language of political science—is not a *Bundesstaat*. Even in English the word *Federation* has a meaning. It means that several distinct political communities agree to become one political community for certain purposes, and to remain distinct political communities for certain other purposes. They agree that each community shall settle its internal affairs for itself, but that common affairs shall be settled by a common power in which all the members are represented. What are to be looked on as internal and what as common affairs must be settled by agreement in each case. The federal ideal is satisfied if there are some things which each State does for itself and some others which the Union does for all. That the Union only should be able to act in international affairs seems essential.* If a man talks about "Imperial Federation," he should tell us whether this is the relation that he proposes to establish, and between what constituent members he proposes to establish it.

Now the paper by Sir John Colomb, headed a "Survey

* It is essential to the *Bundesstaat*; it does not seem to be essential to the *Staatenbund*.

of Existing Conditions," is in many ways a relief to one
who has been greatly puzzled by vague talk. Sir John
Colomb asks, "What is the empire of Her Britannic
Majesty?" To this question the obvious answer is,
"The Empire of India, and nothing else;" for nowhere
else has the word "empire" any legal meaning. Sir
John Colomb talks a good deal about "empire," but
very little about "imperial," and nothing at all about
"Imperial Federation." The name in short is dropped,
and we get "Britannic Confederation" instead. This
certainly makes things a little clearer. There is one
gain at least if "Britannic" is put instead of "Imperial." "Britannic" does suggest "National Unity"
in some shape or other. "Imperial" shuts out
national unity; there is no national unity where one
State exercises lordship or "empire" over another.
Still, the name "Britannic" has an odd sound. It is
unknown except in the formula "Her Britannic
Majesty," meaning the Queen of Great Britain and
Ireland. The word "Britannic" is used only in this
formal diplomatic style. For we talk of "British
Government," "British dominions," "British interests,"
"British Consulate," even "British Ambassador" and
"British Legation." We never, in English at least,
say "Britannic Government" or "Britannic Legation."
But the use of the word "Britannic" at all events
settles at once all difficulties about the "English-
speaking people." The word "English" takes in the
United States, or it ought to do so. The word "Britannic" assuredly does not, any more than the word
"British." And it would be hard to believe that
a "Britannic Confederation" could be meant to take
in that large majority of Her Majesty's subjects

D

who have nothing to do with federation or with freedom in any shape, but who inhabit Her Majesty's Imperial dominion in Asia. We are relieved from all those "imperial" dangers at page 4 of Sir John Colomb's paper. While "Imperial Federation" has never been intelligibly defined, one side of "Britannic Confederation" is very intelligibly defined there. The Empire of India is distinctly shut out. It is not to be in any way federalised; the only question about it is whether it shall be "governed by the United Kingdom or by an united empire." An empire to be governed by another empire, an empire seemingly not united to be governed by another empire which is united, is a little puzzling. But we need not exercise ourselves in such great matters as empires. "Britannic Confederation" is defined to be an union of "the United Kingdom of Great Britain and Ireland, British North America, British South Africa, and Australasia." The West Indies and one or two other British Dependencies seem here to be shut out; but, at any rate, with this definition we at least know where we are.

The terms of the union we are not told; but, as the word "confederation" is used, I conceive that they are meant to be strictly federal. That is to say, first of all, the Parliament of the United Kingdom will give up its right to legislate for British North America, British South Africa, and Australasia. Then the United Kingdom, British North America, British South Africa, and Australasia will enter into a federal relation with one another. They may enter either as single members (States or Cantons) or as groups of members. That is, Great Britain and Ireland might enter as a single State of the Confederation, or England, Scotland, Ireland,

Wales—or possibly smaller divisions again—might enter
as separate States. Or Great Britain, Australia, Canada,
&c., might enter as themselves Leagues, members of a
greater League, as in the old state of things in Graubünden. I am not arguing for or against any of these
arrangements. I am only stating them as possible.
But whatever the units are to be—Great Britain and
Australia, England and Victoria, or anything larger or
smaller—if the Confederation is to be a real one, each
State must keep some powers to itself, and must yield
some powers to a central body. That Central body, in
which all the States must be represented in some way
or other, will naturally deal with all international
matters, all matters that concern the Britannic Confederation as a whole. The legislatures of Great Britain
and Australia, England and Victoria, or whatever the
units fixed on may be, will deal only with the internal
affairs of those several cantons.

Now such a scheme as this is theoretically possible.
That is, it involves no contradiction in terms, as the
talk about Imperial Federation does. It is purely
federal; there is nothing "imperial" about it. It is
simply applying to certain political communities a
process which has been actually gone through by certain
other political communities. It is proposing to recon-
struct a certain political constitution after the model of
certain other political constitutions which are in actual
working. It is therefore something better than mere
talk and theory. But, because it is theoretically possible, it does not follow that it is practically possible,
that is, that it is possible in this particular case. That
a certain system exists, that it has succeeded, in certain
cases, proves only that it *may* succeed in another case;

it does not prove that it *will* succeed. It proves that there is no obvious absurdity in suggesting it, that the suggestion is fairly entitled to be weighed, and, if need be, answered; but it proves nothing more. In each case we must look to the probabilities of the particular case, both political and physical. For this is assuredly a case in which geography has something to say. It is one in which it seems to depend wholly on geographical considerations whether the scheme is likely to succeed or not. If Canada or Australia joined Great Britain, or lay close to Great Britain, the only question would be between absorption and federation. Lying as they do at a great distance, we have ruled that national unity would not be promoted by their absorption into the United Kingdom; we have now to consider whether it is likely to be promoted by their federation.

Of the federations existing at this time the two chief are Switzerland and the United States of America. They differ in this point, that one is very large and the other very small; they agree in this, that the territory of both is continuous. But the proposed Britannic Confederation will be scattered, scattered over every part of the world. I know of no example in any age of a scattered confederation, a scattered *Bundesstaat*. The Hanse Towns were not a *Bundesstaat;* they were hardly a *Staatenbund*. Of the probable working of such a body as that which is now proposed the experience of history can teach us nothing; we can only guess what may be likely. The Britannic Confederation will have its federal congress sitting somewhere, perhaps at West-minster, perhaps at Melbourne, perhaps at some Wash-ington called specially into being at some point more central than either. We are sometimes told that modern science has annihilated time and space; and for some purposes it is so. I have been told that it takes no longer to get to Westminster from the most distant British colonies than, at the time of the union of England and Scotland, it took to come from Shetland to Westminster. May I be allowed to leave out Shetland, which has a case of its own, and to draw the line at Caithness, or to substitute one of the Western Islands for Shetland? Certainly in the days of Queen Anne both those islands and the mainland of Caithness were a very long way from Westminster, perhaps as far, by the almanac, as any Colony is now. Still, from Caithness a man could walk to Westminster; even from the Islands he could get there without crossing or going near any foreign territory. Between Caithness and Westminster there was doubtless on both sides a good deal of traditional ignorance and traditional dislike; but it was the kind of ignorance and dislike which might in time die out, and which largely has died out. It was a wholly different feeling from the feeling of a young dependency which wishes to love the mother-country as long as it is allowed, but which daily feels more and more sharply any sign of inferiority to the mother-country. For a while their representatives will think it grand to sit at Westminster; presently, as the spirit of equality grows, they are not unlikely to ask for some more central place; they may even refuse to stir out of their own territory. That is to say, they will find that the sentiment of national unity, which they undoubtedly have in no small measure, needs some physical and some political basis to stand on. It is hard to believe that States which are united only by a sentiment, which have so much, both political and physical,

to keep them asunder, will be kept together for ever by
a sentiment only. And we must further remember that
that sentiment is a sentiment for the mother-country,
and not for one another. Sir John Macdonald said that
he was born a British subject and that he would die
one. His heart would hardly have been so stirred by
any sentiment of federal brotherhood towards Australia
or South Africa. Canada and Australia care a great
deal for Great Britain; we may doubt whether, apart
from Great Britain, Canada and Australia care very
much for one another. There may be American States
which care yet less for one another; but in their case
mere continuity produces a crowd of interests and relations common to all. We may doubt whether the confederation of States so distant as the existing colonies
of Great Britain, whether the bringing them into closer
relations with one another as well as with Great Britain,
will at all tend to the advance of a common national
unity among them. We may doubt whether it will not
be likely to bring out some hidden tendencies to dis-
union among them.

The ground—a just and natural ground—which makes
a colony wish to get rid of the dependent relation is that
it does not like to be ordered about in any matter by
the Colonial Office at home. It does not like the chance
of being drawn by the mother-country into some relation, perhaps some war, in which it has no interest.
It may be doubted whether a federal relation will practically make matters better in this respect. In form of
course it will do so; each colony will be represented in
the federal body, which will see to all matters of common
interest. But let us look at it in another way. There
is every chance that the federal power, executive and

legislative, will meddle a great deal more with local affairs than the Colonial Office does now. It will do so for the very reason that each colony will be represented in it. It will not, like the Colonial Office, be shy of meddling. The Colonial Office, after all, steps in only now and then, in this and that special case. But if a regular Britannic Confederation be set up, it will be like other confederations. Its Executive branch must be always at work; its Legislative branch must be at work for the same kind of time that other Parliaments and Congresses are at work. It will be inclined to meddle; it will be pressed to meddle; it will be its duty to meddle. It must, in the nature of things, exercise a far greater control over each State than the Colonial Office now does. And though each State will have a voice in it, each State will always be liable to be out-voted on the matters which are dearest to its heart. The interests and feelings of a number of distant and isolated States, none of which will have any particular reason for dealing tenderly with one another, are likely to clash with one another much oftener and much more roughly than happens between particular colonies and a mother-country which has every reason to deal tenderly with all. All these tendencies are present in all confederations; they are the weak side of confederations. But they are likely to come out far more strongly in a confederation of scattered and distant members than they do when the States form a continuous territory. And in the scattered confederation all questions and parties are likely to be local. It is hard to see what will be the materials for the formation of great national parties among such scattered elements.

And one thing more must be said from the side of

the mother-country itself. Does every one who talks about federation, " Imperial," " Britannic," or any other, always think what any kind of federation means as regards the Parliament of Great Britain? We are used to boast that that Parliament knows no superior on Earth, that its powers are limited only by the physical powers of nature. Make Great Britain a member, make England and Scotland separate members, of a Britannic Confederation, and all this greatness passes away. The powers of the British, English, Scottish, Parliament will at once cease to be boundless; they will be cut down to the measure of such powers as the Federal Constitution may leave to each of the several States. The British, English, Scottish, Parliament will sink to the level of the Legislature of Delaware or the Grand Council of Zug. Are we ready for this? I can speak for one man only. I am no lover of "empire"; I am not anxious for my country to exercise lordship over other lands, English-speaking or otherwise. But I will not, so far as one man can hinder it, have my country ruled over by any other power, even by a power in which my country itself has a voice. If it be proposed that the great and historic assembly which King Edward called into existence in 1295 shall keep its six hundredth anniversary by sinking to the level of the Legislature of a Canton of a Britannic Confederation, then I shall be driven, however much against the grain, to turn Jingo and sing " Rule Britannia."

EDWARD A. FREEMAN.

III.

THE COMMERCE OF THE BRITISH EMPIRE.

(*With Diagrams.*)

By GEORGE G. CHISHOLM, M.A., B.Sc.

THE COMMERCE OF THE BRITISH EMPIRE.

IT is natural that in any scheme of federation among members of the British Empire the question of closer commercial union should take a prominent place. The importance of commercial interests to the life of any country at once suggests the idea of a Customs Union as an accompaniment of political federation. The idea is likewise supported by historical examples. The federation of the United States brings with it internal Free Trade for a population of more than sixty millions over an unbroken area of more than three millions of square miles. In the smaller Swiss Confederation there is the same commercial unity. The European empire which, if not properly a federation, as Professor Freeman tells us, most closely simulates one, is nearly conterminous with the German Customs Union. There is a common Customs barrier also for the loose confederation of Austria-Hungary together with Bosnia, Herzegovina, and the principality of Liechtenstein. Internal Free Trade likewise holds good in the great federation already existing within the British Empire—the Dominion of Canada; and it is one of the most important articles in the scheme drawn up as the basis of the proposed federation of the Australasian Colonies.

A Customs Union for the British Empire is therefore, at least, an aspiration naturally associated with the first suggestion of Britannic Confederation. Whether such an union is practicable is a question for the future. That it is essential to any scheme of confederation few, I think, would contend. In the case of the British Empire, as pointed out by Sir John Colomb in the first paper of this series, there are undoubtedly great obstacles in the way. Whether these can be met by any practicable tariff arrangement (either in the way of increased freedom or increased restriction of trade) it is fortunately not my business to consider, since the question of Tariffs, as they affect international commerce, falls to be dealt with by another of the contributors to this series. I would only say here that any attempt on the part of the mother-country to bring about closer commercial relations with the self-governing Colonies by artificial means, contrary to their real interests, would be a vain endeavour. It would have no permanent tendency to promote federation. If political federation demands any sacrifice on the part of either the mother-country or the Colonies, the nature and extent of the sacrifice must be fully understood and fairly recognised on both sides.

In this paper, accordingly, I propose to consider in the briefest manner possible the salient features of the commerce of the principal members of the British Empire as that commerce exists at present,* and to draw attention here and there to such indications as seem to me to be afforded of the present tendencies of

---

* As, from want of space, many points of interest with regard to the trade of the Empire are here passed over, I should like to take this opportunity of drawing attention to a paper on "Inter-

the commercial development. To a solution of the
problem of knitting the Empire together in closer
commercial bonds, this is only a small contribution ;
but such an examination of the actual facts appeared
to me the best preparation I could make for the further
consideration of the question.   In this survey, I have,
of course, included India, for, whatever place may be
assigned to that dependency in a scheme of Britannic
Confederation, its commercial relations must certainly
be a matter of the greatest importance.

In Plates I.–III. are three diagrams, which I have
drawn up to show the proportion which the trade of
the United Kingdom with the Colonial and other
Possessions in the aggregate, as well as with certain
groups of these Possessions, has borne to the whole
trade in each year since 1861. For comparison, I
give here the average annual value in millions and
decimals of millions of pounds of the total trade of the
United Kingdom, under various heads, for the six
periods of five years embraced by the thirty years to
which the diagrams relate :—

	1861–5.	1866–70.	1871–5.	1876–80.	1881–5.	1886–90.
Imports	247.6	292.8	360.2	382.5	399.9	389.6
Gross Exports	190.8	234.7	297.7	258.0	295.3	298.5
Exports of British and Irish Produce and Manufactures	144.4	187.8	239.5	201.4	232.3	236.3

It must be remembered that these figures do not

British Trade and its Influence on the Unity of the Empire," by C.
E. Howard Vincent, C.B., M.P., read at a meeting of the Royal
Colonial Institute on the 12th of May 1890, in which details of
importance are given concerning the trade of each of the Colonies.

show the growth in volume of British commerce during the period. The great rise in prices of many important commodities about 1872-73, and the great fall in prices subsequently, cause them to be misleading in this respect. The actual growth in volume, even in years in which there was a reduction in value, has been shown in one way by Mr. Giffen,* and in another way by Sir Rawson Rawson,† who takes the tonnage of ships entering and clearing at British ports as a rough gauge of the volume of the commerce. Unfortunately the mode in which our shipping statistics are collected does not allow this method to afford such precise results from this point of view as the corresponding statistics of Italy, in which the amount of cargo loaded and discharged at each Italian port is entered.

But, notwithstanding the fact that the figures above given represent inadequately the growth in the total volume of British trade, they indicate at least a very large increase in the total trade within the period; and perhaps the most striking thing brought out by the diagrams in Plates I.-III. is, that through all these changes in the actual amount of the trade, the proportion falling to the Colonies and other Possessions, collectively, has varied within small limits. In the total imports, the extreme limits of variation under this head are 21.1 and 34.1 per cent.; the gross exports to the Colonies and Dependencies were never less than 19.6 per cent., never more than 31.5 per cent.; the exports

* See " Report to the Secretary of the Board of Trade on Recent Changes in the Prices of Exports and Imports " [C. 5386] 1888.

† See the " Sequel to Synopsis of the Tariffs and Trade of the British Empire," by Sir Rawson W. Rawson, K.C.M.G., C.B., published by the Imperial Federation League; and also each number of the *Journal* of the League.

of British produce and manufactures never lower than 23 per cent., never higher than 36.6 per cent.

These figures of course imply that, throughout, the great bulk of our trade has been with foreign countries, and the aggregate of that trade has varied within limits as narrow. They show what a formidable thing it would be to attempt any serious diversion of that trade. When we consider particulars. the appearance of difficulty in this task is only increased. In losing our exports to the United States, for example, we should lose our best market for linen and jute manufactures and for earthenware, one of our best markets for woollen and worsted tissues, and for mixed silk fabrics, and a market of importance for a multitude of other products. In losing our exports to Germany, we should lose our best market for woollen yarn. Coal, which is estimated to form the cargo of considerably more than two-fifths of the tonnage of vessels clearing with cargoes from the United Kingdom,* has a comparatively limited sale in the British Colonies. India and Ceylon are the only two Dependencies which take any considerable quantity, and the export to India is not increasing. As regards imports into the United Kingdom, corn and raw cotton are the two principal articles for which increased sources of supply would have to be found in our Colonies or Dependencies if our trade with foreign countries were restricted in their favour. Already there is a tendency in favour of an increased proportion of wheat and flour being supplied by members of the Empire.† But

---

* See Sir Rawson Rawson's corrected estimate in the July number of the *Journal of the Imperial Federation League.*

† Even this tendency is doubtful. It is not borne out by the statistics furnished to our own import tables for the last five years

no such tendency can be detected in the case of cotton.

Before leaving the general consideration of the diagrams in Plates I.-III., we may note that it is as a market for British produce and manufactures that the Colonies and Dependencies take the most important place in the trade of the United Kingdom. Their share of that commerce is considerably larger than their share

(1886-90) as compared with the previous five. The following figures give the percentage of the total quantity of wheat and flour imported into the United Kingdom from British territory in the four successive periods of five years from 1871 to 1890 :—11.0, 14.5, 21.0, 18.3. In spite of the decline in the last period the statement in the text is, however, probably warranted by the considerations subsequently adduced as to the real growth in the exports of wheat from Canada and the probable development of the wheat trade in North America generally (pp. 72-73), and by the fact that railways have not yet done all that may be expected of them in the way of increasing the wheat supply from India. But on the other side one has to note that of late years Australasia has not been able to keep up the amount of its wheat supplies in the British market, whereas Rumania and the Argentine Republic have been rapidly increasing theirs. In any case the above figures show that to make the United Kingdom independent of foreign wheat a new origin would have to be found for four-fifths of the total external supplies. One other fact is, however, worth noting with respect to this branch of our trade. The period 1886-90 was the first of the successive periods of equal length from the middle of the century (and even earlier) in which the aggregate import of wheat and flour was less than in the previous period, as is shown by the following figures, giving the average annual imports of wheat and flour in millions and decimals of millions of cwts. in each of the periods from 1851-55 downwards, one cwt. of flour being reckoned as equal to $1\frac{1}{4}$ cwt. of wheat, as is done in the *Agricultural Returns* of the United Kingdom :—20.11, 23.59, 34.65, 37.27, 50.49, 63.31, 76.78, 75.93. From these figures one may not unreasonably infer that the United Kingdom is one part of British territory that may expect to supply the home market in future years with a greater proportion of wheat.

in the general exports, and still more in excess of their
share in the imports of the United Kingdom.

If, instead of examining the trade returns of the
United Kingdom, we study those of the separate Colonies
and Dependencies, we find that the trade with the United
Kingdom is to them relatively of much more value than
the aggregate of their trade is to us. In nearly every
case we find that the United Kingdom takes the first
place both in exports and imports, and in many cases
the bulk of the trade is with the home-country. This
is not surprising. The Colonies and Dependencies may
for the most part be classed either as new countries
engaged in the development of the agricultural resources
of the Temperate zone, or countries supplying Tropical
produce. In either case, Great Britain is in a peculiarly
favourable position for supplying their wants and receiving their products. Its wealth in coal and iron, both
found in the most favourable situations; its crowded
and skilled industrial population, its abundance of easily
accessible seaports, all combine to make Great Britain
better fitted by nature than any other country for supplying the manufactured articles that new countries and
Tropical countries require, and hence also for receiving
their products, whether in the form of raw materials or
articles of food and drink. Moreover, the geographical
position of Great Britain and its other advantages for
shipping render it peculiarly well adapted for the collection of produce from all parts of the World, to be as
widely distributed in other parts—a totally different
thing from the merely transit trade which forms a large
part of the "general" commerce of countries with a
land-frontier. The steadiness of this part of British
trade is well shown by the following figures, which

E

give the percentage value of the exports of foreign and
Colonial produce to the total value of British exports
for periods of five years :—

Years	1861-5	1866-70	1871-5	1876-80	1881-5	1886-90
Per cent.	24.4	20.0	19.5	21.5	21.3	20.84

Of the Colonies in which the trade with the United
Kingdom does not take the leading place, both in imports and exports, the most important is Canada. According to the " Statistical Year-Book for Canada" for
1889, the share of Great Britain and the United States
in the trade with the Dominion in four successive quin-
quennial periods is shown by the following figures :—

Imports into Canada for Home Consumption.

	1868-72 Per cent.	1873-77 Per cent.	1878-82 Per cent.	1883-87 Per cent.
From Great Britain	55.46	48.13	44.03	41.25
„ United States	35.08	44.24	46.18	45.18

Exports of Canadian Produce.

To Great Britain	37.53	47.68	47.96	46.62
„ United States	51.50	41.31	41.76	44.41

In the year ending 30th June 1889 the proportions
were :—Imports from Great Britain, 38.68; from the
United States, 46.07 per cent. Exports to Great
Britain, 43.12; to the United States, 46.91 per cent.

The magnitude of the Canadian trade makes these
figures all the more worth inquiring into. Let us consider, then, the principal articles in which the trade
with these two countries is carried on. Among the

articles imported in greater quantity from the United States than from elsewhere, are bituminous coal and anthracite, mineral and lubricating oils, raw cotton, maize, wheat flour, hops, meats of all sorts, and other kinds of agricultural produce of the country; raw silk, coffee, and crude rubber, among the produce of foreign countries; copper and copper wire, and, among manufactured articles, agricultural implements, locomotive engines, and some other products of the iron industry, sole leather and boots and shoes, certain varieties of cotton, glass, and paper manufactures, besides others of less importance. Under the head of exports sent chiefly to the United States, we find various products of the lumber industry—that is, wooden articles worked up into such a form as to be ready or nearly ready for use, such as laths, joists, shingles, sleepers, shocks, &c., whereas Canadian forest produce is sent to the United Kingdom more largely in the form of deals and square timber. Then we find among animals chiefly sent to the United States, horses and sheep; amongst other agricultural produce, barley, eggs, potatoes, and hides, horns, and skins other than fur. Among mineral products, that which is chiefly sent to the United States is coal. Of the products of the fisheries, smoked herrings are principally sent to the United States, dry salted cod and pickled herring mainly to the British West Indies and the United States, fresh salmon to the United States, canned salmon to the United Kingdom, canned lobsters about equally to both countries. Tanning bark —that is, principally the bark of the hemlock pine—is sent mostly to the United States; extract of hemlock bark (for tanning) mostly to the United Kingdom.

Now, in reviewing such lists as the foregoing, taking

into consideration the diverse products of the two countries and the mutual relations of their more populous parts, one is disposed to ask with regard to the imports, Where else could they come from? with regard to the exports, Where else could they go to?

A closer examination of the trade between Canada and the United States gives strong support to the contention of Mr. Goldwin Smith that the scattered populations of the Dominion naturally seek to carry on commerce with four different sections of the United States. The maritime provinces of Canada and the States of New England, together with the eastern portions of the States immediately to the south of New England, have an obvious interest in exchanging their products. Ontario and Quebec are naturally anxious to trade with the States adjacent to the parts containing the bulk of their population—that is, with New York, Pennsylvania, Ohio, and Michigan. As regards Manitoba, again, no doubt Great Britain forms, as things now are, the best market for the bulk of its produce; but, on the other hand, it is natural that the province should desire to buy its agricultural implements and supply many of its other wants through the great mercantile agencies of St. Paul. Finally, the Pacific States of the Union are the natural market, almost the sole market of importance, for some of the principal products of British Columbia, and the natural source of supply of some of the chief wants of that province.

To establish these facts by an analysis of the trade between Canada and the United States (so far as the trade-returns of the two countries enable us to make such an analysis) would occupy too much of our space, but a few illustrations of the grounds for Mr. Goldwin

Smith's contention may be adduced with advantage. We may notice in the first place that in the case of coal the United States stand first both in supplying this commodity to Canada and in receiving it from Canada. But the coal which Canada receives from the United States, partly in the form of dutiable bituminous coal, partly in the form of duty-free anthracite, is mostly imported into Ontario and Quebec,* which are not coal-producing provinces. That which Canada supplies to the United States is mainly sent from British Columbia to California, a State which does not produce one-tenth of a ton of coal per head for its own population. The Pacific coast of the United States forms, in fact, the principal market for British Columbian coal, taking at least seven-eighths of the whole production. To withdraw this market accordingly would be to destroy the industry.

Take, again, the petroleum products. Where should we expect Canada to make good the deficiency of her own supplies under this head except in the United States, seeing that one of the two great petroleum-producing regions of the World lies in that country, not far from her own borders and within easy reach of the bulk of her population?

Though both countries are in the main agricultural, they are fitted by nature to supply each other with

* All but a small fraction of the bituminous coal is imported into the province of Ontario, Quebec being able to supply itself easily enough from Nova Scotia, and receiving, in certain years at least, more bituminous coal from Great Britain than from the United States, though the import from Great Britain into the Dominion is only a trifling fraction of the whole supply. From the United States, however, Quebec receives large supplies of anthracite, though not so large a quantity as Ontario.

agricultural products, some of which are most advantageously produced in the one country, others in the other. Confining our attention to the cooler parts of the Temperate zone—that is, to the products of Canada and that part of the United States which lies nearest the Canadian border—we find that the United States are able to supply to Canada, for home consumption, enormous quantities of maize and maize (corn) meal, wheat flour, pork, bacon and hams, beef, lard and tallow. Canada, on the other hand, is able to supply to the United States enormous quantities of barley and eggs, and larger quantities of peas, apples, and potatoes, greater numbers of sheep, cattle, and horses, than are imported into Canada from the United States. The Canadian barley is mainly exported from Ontario, which supplies the barley most esteemed in United States breweries. The eggs are sent most largely from the same province and Prince Edward Island; and how much this trade meets the requirements of natural conditions is shown by the fact that, in the year ending 30th June 1889, a year in which eggs were admitted duty free into both countries, the export of eggs from Canada to the United States was more than twenty times as great as the import from the United States into Canada.

Now, in the circumstances that are merely illustrated, and by no means fully indicated, by these facts, we need not wonder that the trade between the United States and Canada has shown a decided tendency to increase, and even that it has in recent years been increasing at a more rapid rate relatively than the trade with the mother-country. Moreover, this trade, so far as it has been illustrated above, is not one upon which the

mother-country can look with any feeling of regret.
It is in no way prejudicial to us, and if it were stopped
or hindered, we could only deplore the blow thus in-
flicted on Canada as part of the British Empire. The
Canadian coal is not wanted by us, and there is no other
part of the Empire that could take it in any great
quantity. Australia not only supplies all her own wants
in coal, but already takes a share in supplying the
market of San Francisco. We are utterly unable to
supply our own requirements in mineral oil, and are
thus incompetent to make good the deficiencies of
Canada. We are glad to take Canadian timber, cheese,
butter, and wheat; but now that the exports of barley,
eggs, potatoes, &c., from Canada to the United States
are struck at by the M'Kinley tariff, the British market
will be able to make good to Canada the loss thus caused
only to a very limited extent. At present Canada supplies Great Britain (at least directly) only with the
most insignificant fraction of the barley which we import. Potatoes will not bear the cost of a long transit
unless they are such as bring an exceptionally high
price, and eggs also for the most part seek the nearest
available market. Canada perhaps cannot send us too
much canned salmon, but if Canadian fresh salmon were
shut out of the United States, that would be of no
advantage to us, and merely an injury to the people of
both the United States and Canada.

We may repeat, then, that the vigorous growth of the
trade between Canada and the United States need not
be a matter of wonder to anybody, nor of regret on our
part. It is no less surprising that the people of Canada
should desire to have their trade relations with their
great neighbour as intimate as possible.

Moreover, if any forecast as to the future tendencies of commercial development between the two countries may be attempted, it seems to me that the geographical relations between them, and their recent economic history, both warrant us in anticipating an increasing need of each other's products on the part of the two countries. Consider first the unparalleled rapidity with which the coal and iron production of the United States has been growing in recent years, in consequence of which the United States production of iron has already overtaken that of the United Kingdom, and its production of coal may be expected likewise to exceed the British production within no long time. Beyond all question this rapid development in the production of the two most useful minerals implies a correspondingly rapid expansion of manufacturing industries generally in the United States. That such an expansion has in fact taken place is indeed notorious, and statistics show that the agricultural industry of the country, or at least that branch of it which is concerned in supplying the chief food-grain of the manufacturing population, has not kept pace with this growth. For about ten years the wheat area of the United States has been almost stationary. Though still able to supply all its own population with wheat, and to afford a large surplus for export, the amount of this surplus shows a tendency to diminish. "The truth of the matter is," to use the words of Dr. Longstaff, "that while the railway and the 'self-binder' have been increasing so largely the wheat supply, a vast city population has been growing up in the eastern and middle States, a population as dependent on imports of food as any in Europe." * Now

* "Studies in Statistics," p. 188.

whereas, with regard to wheat, the United States show
a diminishing exporting power, Canada shows the
opposite. While many parts of the World in consequence of the recent rapid fall in the price of wheat
have manifested a tendency to contract their area under
that crop, Canada contains in the province of Manitoba
one of those regions in which an expansion of the wheat
area has gone on unchecked.* Manitoba and the Canadian North-West generally probably embrace indeed
the largest area, at least in the New World, in which
wheat cultivation may be extended with success for a
considerable time to come—the most extensive still-
unoccupied area suited for settlement by the vigorous
populations of Northern Europe. Since the Dominion
came into existence it has passed from the list of
countries in which the wheat imports exceed the exports to that in which the wheat exports exceed the
imports. In the five years 1870–74 the Dominion imported an excess of wheat and wheat flour amounting in
all to $5\frac{1}{4}$ million bushels; in the five years 1885–89 it
exported an excess of $14\frac{1}{2}$ million bushels derived from
Canadian fields. It is true that only an insignificant
proportion of this export is destined for the United
States, but if the facts to which attention has just been
drawn may be taken to indicate tendencies favoured by
natural conditions (which seems actually to be the case),
we may reasonably anticipate that in no long time it
will be otherwise. We may expect that in the future
the manufacturing populations of the north-eastern
section of the United States will look to the Canadian
North-West for a large part of their wheat supply,

* The area under wheat in Manitoba increased year by year from
51,000 acres in 1881 to 917,000 acres in 1891.

just as inevitably as the manufacturing populations of Western Europe. On the other hand the middle provinces of Canada will still find themselves most conveniently supplied with coal, petroleum, and probably many other commodities, by the United States.

Considering, moreover, the enormous undeveloped resources of Canada, both mineral and other, we cannot but admit that if there were Free Trade with the United States an important and healthy stimulus would be given to the development of these resources, provided that it did not hamper the commerce of the country in other ways; and, keeping that fact in view, we can hardly be surprised that there should be a strong and active party in Canada crying out for reciprocity with the United States at any cost—even at the cost, which at the present juncture would be unavoidable, of discriminating strongly against the products of the mother-country in the Canadian markets. But however natural the cry may be, its wisdom is by no means so certain. The most intimate commercial relations with the United States may be of the utmost advantage to Canada when secured without other disadvantages, but it does not follow that the people of the Dominion would find their advantage in establishing such relations by subjecting themselves, for example, to a tariff that would weigh heavily upon the agricultural population—that is, the majority of the inhabitants of the country—and, moreover, would render all the industries of the country subject to the caprice of a foreign government to a much greater extent than can possibly be the case as long as it remains master of its own fiscal system.

As regards Newfoundland, the only other important North American Colony, the great bulk of the export

trade of this island has always been with the great
Roman Catholic consumers of fish—Portugal and other
Mediterranean countries in Europe, Brazil in South
America. Frequently, however, the United Kingdom
stands first, even under this heading, among the individual countries. In former years it was always first.
On the import side the great bulk of the Newfoundland
trade is with members of the Empire, principally the
United Kingdom and Canada. Under both heads,
however, the United States are naturally prominent,
especially under that of imports. As a market for fresh
fish they would undoubtedly be of much greater importance but for tariff restrictions.

Let us turn now to Australia and New Zealand, the
most important of all the Colonial groups furnishing
(besides minerals) principally products of the Temperate
zone. Of all our Colonies these are the most completely
British as regards the composition of their population.
At the same time, they are among those whose trade
with the mother-country stands relatively highest. In
all these Colonies the great bulk of the external trade
is either with the mother-country or with each other,
and, if we disregard the merely transit trade between the
different Colonies, the trade with the United Kingdom
constitutes by far the largest share of the whole. So far
all seems satisfactory. But if we look at the lines in
our export diagram showing the proportion of British
exports to these Colonies, we notice that after a long
period in which these lines show a very encouraging rise,
they have at last begun to droop. This may not mean
very much. It may only mean that in the last few years
the trade with other countries has advanced somewhat
more rapidly than that with Australasia. It does not

necessarily imply any decline, or even arrest of growth in our Australasian trade. But when we consider the total value of British trade with these Colonies, we find that in the aggregate of the five years 1886–90 there has been a decline of $6\frac{1}{2}$ millions sterling in the value of the exports of British produce and manufactures, and that this decline has not been even partially compensated by any increase in the exports from the United Kingdom of foreign and Colonial produce, for these show an additional decline of more than half a million. A further examination of this trade with the aid of Colonial statistics brings out results even less satisfactory from the British point of view, for we find that, while the British trade with these Colonies has been declining, the foreign trade with them has been growing. The Australasian imports from the United Kingdom sank from an annual average of £30.71 millions in 1881–85 to £28.78 millions in 1886–89, the Australasian exports to the United Kingdom sank in the same period from an annual average of £25.93 millions to £25.68; but the imports of these Colonies from foreign countries rose in the corresponding periods from an average of £5.06 to one of £5.59, their exports to foreign countries from an average of £2.57 to £2.93 millions.

An examination of the trade returns of the individual Colonies reveals the fact that in the trade with the United Kingdom a large rise in the imports into Victoria and smaller advances in the imports into Queensland and Western Australia are more than counterbalanced by a decline in the case of the other Colonies—above all, New South Wales; and that in the exports to the United Kingdom, both the leading Colonies exhibit a decline (Victoria much the greater), whereas New

Zealand, Queensland, and Western Australia all show a substantial rise.   In the case of Victoria, the principal rise in the imports consisted in metals and machinery, which was, no doubt, connected with another spurt in railway construction and factory building.   On the export side New Zealand showed the most noteworthy rise.   Fresh mutton, hemp, sheepskins, and wool were all despatched thence to the United Kingdom in increased quantity in the second period, the fresh mutton trade showing special signs of vigorous development.

In the trade with foreign countries we may note particularly the share belonging to the two leading Colonies.   Under the head of imports a large rise (averaging nearly £0.7 million per annum) more than makes up for a fall in the case of New South Wales (on the average less than £60,000).   Germany, Sweden and Norway, Belgium and France, and the United States all shared in this rise.   Under the head of exports a large rise in New South Wales (averaging about £0.33 million) is partly counterbalanced only by a very trifling decline in Victoria.   The rise in this case is mainly due to an increased export of wool to Germany, of gold coin, coal, and tin to the United States.

The growth of the trade with Germany is specially worthy of attention.   It may be said to date from 1879, when the North German Lloyd's line of steamers began to run between Hamburg and Sydney.   Since that year the imports from Germany into New South Wales have increased, in every year except two, from £32,000 to upwards of £500,000 in 1889; the exports to Germany from less than £5000 to about the same value as the imports.   In the Victorian trade with Germany the value of the imports advanced between the same dates with even greater steadiness from £16,000, to more than £600,000, that of the exports to Germany from less than £1000 to upwards of £200,000. In both Colonies this trade made a great upward bound in 1889, for in the latter part of 1888 it was further stimulated by the establishment of a line of German cargo boats to open up communication between the great wool-exporting cities of Sydney and Melbourne, as well as Adelaide, and the ports of Bremen and Antwerp.

We have already noted that the increased export from New South Wales to Germany consists chiefly of wool, and the rise in this export demands particular consideration. From the peculiar advantages which enormous areas in Australasia possess for the production of excellent wool and for the production of little else, this export may probably be safely regarded as a permanent feature, and a permanent feature of the greatest importance, in Australasian trade. Ten years ago practically the whole of the wool exported from these Colonies was sent, in the first instance, to Great Britain (principally to London), but a large portion of it has always been re-exported to foreign countries. For about twenty years, indeed, wool has been the principal article of foreign or Colonial origin exported from the United Kingdom, and the rapid rise in the absolute value of this export has till within the last two or three years served to make good the loss in the British re-export trade traceable to the opening of the Suez Canal and other causes. But this trade seems at last to be threatened. Germany is not the only country that now buys wool in increasing quantity direct from Australasia. Antwerp, Havre, and Dunkirk share this trade with Bremen and Hamburg. The

total value of wool directly exported to Continental
ports increased from £172,000 in 1881 to £1,557,000
in 1888.

This diversion of trade appears to be principally due
to causes over which we have no control.* We are
already in the most favourable position for acting as
the intermediaries in this trade. The growth of the
direct trade with the Continent is likely to stimulate
the demand for Australasian wool, and the Australian
Colonies therefore would probably resent proposals
designed to aid the mother-country in retaining this
trade by artificial means.† The larger the direct trade
with the Continent grows, the more likely is it to be
carried on with increasing success. London still retains
immense advantages as the great wool-market of the
world in which wools of all kinds can be sorted, mixed,
and graded, and in which accordingly the buyer has the
best chance of getting exactly what he wants. But if
the direct trade of Australasia with the Continental
wool-ports (which already receive the bulk of the
Argentine wool) attains such a magnitude as to enable
one or more Continental ports to rival London as a wool-
market, the growth of that direct trade will thereby be
accelerated. In the meantime we can only console
ourselves with the reflection that if we are in the end

---

* It was, however, one of the most serious aspects of the labour
troubles at the London docks two years ago, that they tended to
promote a diversion of trade already in progress from other causes.

† So far, however, as this change in the course of trade is due not
to natural causes but to the artificial stimulus of foreign subsidies,
the endeavour to counteract the effects of such a stimulus artifi-
cially might not indeed be the wisest course to follow, but at least
would not be open to the same objection as an attempt by artificial
means to fight against natural tendencies.

destined to lose this trade the sooner the change begins, and the more gradually it proceeds, the better will it be for us. Continued growth would in the circumstances supposed only lead to a greater loss. According to an alarmist report copied into the *Board of Trade Journal* for May 1891, it was estimated that half the total wool production of the Australian Colonies (or at any rate of the colonies of Victoria, New South Wales, and South Australia—it is not clear which is meant), would be sent direct to the Continent in 1891. A change so sudden would be a disaster to England, or at least to the port of London and the London wool-market. But, occurring at a period when no events took place to interfere with the peaceful development of trade, it would be without a parallel in modern commerce. We may hope, therefore, that the change will proceed with more gradual steps, so that we may be able to accommodate ourselves to it more easily. So far there is no sign of any change so abrupt and violent in our own trade reports, for the returns for the six months ending June 30th 1891 show a substantial increase in our import of wool from Australia over the corresponding period of the two previous years.

The trade with the Cape Colony and Natal need not detain us long. In recent years it presents some encouraging features. Notably these Colonies have of late been growing in relative importance as a market for British produce. In the years 1872 to 1882, we notice the effects of the stimulus given to trade by the working of the Kimberley diamond-field, and after a lull we may notice in more recent years the effect of the similar stimulus arising from the working of the Transvaal gold-fields, much of the produce destined for which passes through the Cape or Natal. As stated in the beginning of this paper it is this rapid development of new countries or new regions that Great Britain is peculiarly fitted to promote, and which accordingly is peculiarly fitted to stimulate British trade. Fortunately for us the favourable accounts given of Matabele and Mashona Lands hold out the prospect of a prolonged stimulation of British commerce from the recent settlements in those regions. As in some cases, however, trade that is really carried on with foreign countries gets entered in our returns as trade with a British Colony,* so it may happen that much of the trade with these new British settlements may appear in these returns as trade with a foreign country.

Passing over the minor Colonies of the Temperate zone, let us now turn our attention to the principal Tropical Colonies and Dependencies. The most important group is of course that of the British East Indies, and the most important constituent of that group, India itself. In several respects the external trade of India is highly remarkable. It consists mainly in the exchange of Tropical and sub-Tropical products of agriculture for manufactured and mineral products of the Temperate zone. By certain economists accordingly its external trade would be regarded as the very ideal of commerce. Its export trade in Tropical and sub-Tropical produce is the largest in the World.

Further, the population of India is the largest in the World whose external trade is regulated on a Free Trade

---

* For that reason a line has been introduced into all our diagrams showing the proportion of trade with the British Colonies and Dependencies, exclusive of that with Hong-Kong, this latter trade being virtually trade with a foreign country.

basis. The officials who control the government of
India being thoroughly imbued with the Free Trade ideas
which dominate the commercial policy of our own
country, have arranged the tariff of India on the same
principle. External trade is not exactly free. There
is still one article (rice) on which an export duty is
levied. But the import tariff is as limited as our own,
and is obviously designed for revenue purposes only.

The increase in the amount and value of the external
trade of India for many years has also been very remarkable, as is shown by the following figures, which
give in millions and decimals of millions of Rx. (tens
of rupees) the average value of the sea-borne trade (the
great bulk of the whole) for periods of five years ending
the 31st of March. The figures relate to merchandise
only, including Government stores, but excluding coin
and bullion :—

	1871-5.	1876-80.	1881-5.	1886-90.
Imports	33.70	39.35	53.06	64.22
Exports	57.02	62 50	82.28	92.68

These figures may be taken as representing fairly well
the growth in volume of the trade of India in the
period, but, owing to the fall in gold prices, including
that of silver, which has taken place in the interval,
they are not suitable for comparison with the figures
given above for the trade of the United Kingdom.
I have accordingly calculated the value of the Indian
trade in pounds sterling, in accordance with the average
rate of exchange of the rupee for each year. The results
here follow :—

Indian Sea-borne Commerce.

Average value in millions and decimals of a million £.

	1871-5.	1876-80.	1881-5.	1886-90.
Imports . .	31.68	33.67	43.40	45.58
Exports . .	53.66	53.42	67.30	65.83

These figures may be compared with those for the
United Kingdom above referred to, and the comparison
shows that in India the advance, on the whole, has
been much greater and much better sustained than in
our own country—a fact by no means surprising when
we consider that within the period in question India
added 11,000 miles to her railway system (thus more
than trebling its length at the beginning of the period),
and that the development of the traffic through the
Suez Canal, which affects a much larger proportion of
the commerce of India than of that of the United
Kingdom, also belongs principally to this period.

Several features of the lines exhibiting the proportion
of the commerce with India in the whole trade of the
United Kingdom are worthy of particular attention.
First, we may note the great rise in the proportion
both of imports from India and exports to India, but
especially in the former, at the beginning of the period
included in our diagrams. This rise belongs to a period
in the history of Indian commerce which illustrates in
a striking manner the disadvantage of having trade
excessively stimulated from temporary causes. The
commerce so created is difficult or impossible to retain.
The prosperity, or apparent prosperity, thus brought
about is invariably followed by a period of adversity,
the character of which differs according to circumstances.
In some cases it may be a period of long and gradual

decline ; in others it may come in the form of sudden
disaster. In the commerce of India the abnormal rise
to which we are now referring was a consequence of the
civil war in America, when the supply of raw cotton
was so greatly reduced that the cultivation of this crop
was entered on with great eagerness in all parts of the
World with a suitable climate and a favourable situation
for exporting the product. India was the country most
powerfully affected by the crisis. Its cotton production
was suddenly increased to an enormous extent. During
the course of the crisis its exporting power was greatly
increased by the completion (in 1863) of the railway
from Bombay up the Bhor Ghát, a railway affording a
greatly improved outlet for the most productive cotton-
growing districts of the Indian table-land. The great
rise in the proportion of the imports from India during
this period was due, not only to the increased amount
of Indian cotton exported to this country, but also to
the rise in value of the commodity. The prosperity
lasted only to the end of the American war. "It led,"
says Sir William Hunter, "to much wild speculation.
The collapse came in 1865. . . . The bubble schemes
and financial companies in Bombay city burst one after
the other, and brought down in the general ruin the
quasi-official Bank of Bombay. In 1865- 66 the quantity
of raw cotton exported was nearly three-fifths more than
in 1864–65, but the total value was about £2,000,000
less. Since 1865–66 the total export of raw cotton from
India has only in one year (1871–72) exceeded the amount
then exported, and in several years it has sunk below
the amount reached before the period of abnormal but
temporary prosperity.

Considered from the British point of view, Indian

trade is, in one respect at least, highly satisfactory.
India is the most important part of the Empire as a
market for British produce.   Plate III. shows a decline
in relative importance in this respect after the abnormal
rise in 1863-64, due indirectly to the same cause as the
rise in the imports from India just considered; but
after 1872 there was, on the whole, a prolonged rise,
and a high relative value has been maintained to the
last.   It must be remembered, moreover, that the
diagrams, exhibiting as they do only relative values,
do not necessarily imply fluctuations in the total actual
value of the trade corresponding with the variations
in the lines there drawn.   To test whether this is so
or not, we must have recourse to the figures showing
the actual values, and when this is done the result turns
out to be more satisfactory than that which seems to
be presented by the diagram now under consideration.
Taking from Indian returns the average of the five
years ending March 31st, 1890, we find that the total
value of the merchandise imported from the United
Kingdom in that period was nearly four-fifths (78.5 per
cent.) of the total value imported from all countries, a
proportion in excess of that of at least the three previous
periods of equal length.   A further examination of the
figures shows, too, that this advance in British commerce
with India is not due to any increased export to India
of foreign and Colonial produce from the United Kingdom.   It shows a real growth in the value of the Indian
market for British produce.

The Import Diagram, Plate I., conveys the impression
of a less satisfactory state of matters from the point of
view of the British merchant, and in this case a closer
study of the figures confirms, and even strengthens, that

impression. In the period of five years ending March
31st, 1875, the value of the exports by sea from British
India was about one-half the total value. In each sub-
sequent period of five years there was a considerable
decline in this proportion until in the last period (ending
March 31st, 1890) the proportion was less than two-
fifths (39.4 per cent.). This cannot be regarded as
anything else than an inevitable consequence of the
opening of the Suez Canal. The Tropical and sub-
Tropical produce of India is of a kind required more or less
in all Temperate countries. Previously to the opening
of the Suez Canal, Great Britain was the one distribut-
ing-centre for this produce. Since that event it has,
however, become less and less so. Much of it is now
discharged directly at Mediterranean ports on the route
from India to Great Britain by way of that canal. The
countries that have thereby principally increased their
direct trade with India hitherto are Egypt, Austria-
Hungary, Italy, and France. In quite recent years
Germany also has greatly increased this branch of its
trade. Though the imports from Germany into India
still remain small, the exports from India to Germany
have increased about sevenfold in the four years 1885–86
to 1886–90—in gold values from about £300,000 to
about £2,000,000. Possibly this result also is one of
the more indirect consequences of the opening of the
Suez Canal. But even though that event has undoubtedly led to the diversion of a certain proportion
of Indian and other commerce from British ports, it is
to be hoped that no one will jump to the conclusion
that it has been, on the whole, injurious to our commerce. It has so greatly increased the magnitude
of international commerce generally that the British

gain therefrom has assuredly been greater than its loss.

So much with regard to the countries trading with India. With respect to the commodities in which Indian trade is carried on there are also one or two matters well worthy of attention. We have said that the exports of India consist mainly of Tropical and sub-Tropical produce. But there are some notable exceptions to this rule. In the first place, there is a large part of India in which the cool season of the year corresponds with the only productive season of certain parts of the Temperate zone, and in which, accordingly, the products of that season are not Tropical. From this region England has, since the beginning of last decade, derived large quantities of wheat, and for a few years the amount of this export increased so rapidly as to excite the greatest alarm among the agricultural population of this country. There is, in fact, no reason to believe that this export has reached its limit, but the statistics of recent years have shown that, at the price to which wheat fell, partly in consequence of this new contribution to the English wheat market, the export from India was not capable of the continuous expansion that was at one time apprehended. Down to 1890, inclusive, the maximum import of Indian wheat into the United Kingdom was that of the year 1885.

Secondly, the export of certain manufactures from India has increased of late years very considerably—in one case with quite remarkable steadiness and rapidity. The export referred to in this case is that of cotton yarn, which is principally sent to China and Japan. It indicates the growth of an industry in direct competition with one of the industries of Lancashire, and the figures showing the severity of this competition are very striking. The export of cotton yarn from British India to the countries mentioned increased year by year, without exception, from somewhat less than 8 million lbs. in the year ending March 31st, 1877, to upwards of 162 million lbs. in the year ending March 31st, 1891. During the same period the amount of the British export of the same commodity to the same destinations varied greatly. It has never reached 48 million lbs., and in recent years it has shown no tendency to increase at all.

Looking to such facts as these, Sir William Hunter has declared that he should not shrink from "the generalisation that the World seemed now to be entering on a new era of competition—the competition between the productive powers of the Tropics and of the Temperate zone."[*] In the case in question, however, it is doubtful whether the greater productiveness of the Tropics is an element in the result at all. The chief factor in favour of India in this commerce appears to be that India not only produces the raw material required for the industry, but also lies much nearer than England to the markets of Eastern Asia. India's main advantage is thus geographical, but not the advantage that it derives from being a Tropical instead of a Temperate country, except in that the raw material in this case happens to be a Tropical or sub-Tropical product.[†] The advantage of India in this case is analogous to that

* Paper on the "Industrial Era in India," by Sir William Hunter, K.C.S.I., &c.: "Proceed. Royal Colonial Inst.," vol. xix. (1887–88), p. 275.

† No doubt India also derives a certain advantage in carrying on this commerce from the fact that Indian trade with China and Japan is free from the uncertainty attaching to the British commerce with these countries, in consequence of the recent changes in

which Scandinavia has for supplying timber products
to Western Europe, and Canada for supplying similar
products to the United States.   The yarn exported by
India is only such as can be made with Indian cotton—
that is, coarse yarns, or " low counts," as they are called
in Lancashire.   While India's export of such yarns has
been growing, and has thus put a check on the growth
of the export of similar yarns of British manufacture,
India's own import of cotton yarn from the United
Kingdom has gone on increasing, and that on the whole
not slowly.   But this increase appears to be in yarns
of a better quality.   Whereas in 1881 the cotton yarn
exported from the United Kingdom to India constituted
15.8 per cent. of the quantity and 19.1 per cent. of the
value of the total British export of this commodity, it
made up in 1890, 19.2 per cent. of the quantity and
25.7 per cent. of the value.   The value of this British
export to India has thus grown at a greater rate relatively than the amount, from which it would appear that
India is now able to buy from the United Kingdom
more expensive yarns than formerly—a fact of no little
significance when we consider the importance of this
commodity in the consumption of the great bulk of the
people.

The only other rising export of importance from India
coming under the head of manufactured articles is that
of leather.   Of the enormous quantities of hides and
skins which India exports, a steadily increasing proportion leaves the country in the dressed or tanned form.

the relative value of gold and silver.   It may be noted, however,
that the Indian exports here spoken of have increased even more
largely in the last two or three years, when the value of silver was
rising, than in previous years, when it was falling.

In this case also geographical facts account for the change. For this trade the advantages which India enjoys are similar to those possessed by the United States—abundant supplies of the raw material and the tanning agents, together with a large industrial population.

But though geographical factors, apart from the greater productiveness of the Tropics, account in a large measure for the growth of Indian manufactures, this greater productiveness is, nevertheless, a fact of the highest importance commercially. It gives rise in the first place to a much greater variety in the products utilisable in commerce whether in the shape of raw materials or articles of food, &c. The Tropics have thus a geographical advantage for a greater number of products than the Temperate zone. It leads also to greater cheapness in the production of food even where the population is dense, and hence causes wages to be relatively lower than in the Temperate zone. It is only in this way that a Tropical situation could tend to give any advantage over other parts of the World in the working of minerals where they happen to exist. But both these advantages would appear to be counter-balanced to a great extent by the diminished energy of the worker in a Tropical climate. As regards wages, it was stated in evidence before the committee of inquiry on Bombay and Lancashire cotton-spinning, appointed by the Manchester Chamber of Commerce, that, relative efficiency being considered, the cost of labour (including the labour of supervision) in Bombay and Lancashire was about equal, and that the wages of Indian operatives increased with their efficiency.* We may hope, there-

* See the Report of this Inquiry, paragraphs 529 and 154-61.

fore, that in the future the greater human energy of the Temperate zone will be the true correlative of the greater productiveness of the Tropics; that the two zones will prove permanently complementary to one another; that, as the products of the Tropics are indispensable to the inhabitants of the Temperate zone, so certain products of the Temperate zone will remain indispensable in the Tropics. Sir William Hunter himself points out that India seems, with the growth of her own manufactures, to have an ever-growing fund for the purchase of goods in England, and he anticipates that in the end the development of the industrial era in India will be a gain to Britain in common with the whole World.

Space forbids our entering at any length on the other Tropical parts of the Empire in the Old World, and to do so would indeed be superfluous for the purpose now in view. The fluctuations in the trade with Ceylon bear witness to the vicissitudes affecting the coffee, tea, cinchona, and other plantations of the Colony; those in the trade with the Straits Settlements afford similar evidence as to the fluctuations in the tin industry of the Malay States, and the entrepôt trade of Singapore. Though the trade of Mauritius with the United Kingdom is relatively small, that trade, nevertheless, furnishes a good illustration of the saying, "Trade follows the flag," inasmuch as the great bulk of it is with other British Possessions, principally India and Australasia. From the Mauritius India derives annually from 50,000 to 60,000 tons of sugar, or even more, and yet it receives only a trifling quantity of any product from the neighbouring island of Réunion, which is all the more striking since it supplies to both islands the bulk of the rice consumed by the plantation labourers.

Our diagrams show the relative importance of our trade with our principal Tropical Possessions in the New World—the British West Indies and Guiana. It is a trade that has suffered more or less in recent years through the competition of foreign countries, stimulated by sugar-bounties. Till recently the trade with the United Kingdom held the first place in the commerce of the principal Colonies, but of late years the growth of the export of sugar from many of them and of fresh Tropical fruits (principally bananas) from Jamaica to the United States has caused the latter country to rise to the first place among those receiving the exports of Jamaica and Barbadoes as well as some of the minor islands. This trade is obviously greatly favoured by the geographical conditions, and it can hardly be doubted that it will tend to grow in the future.

GEORGE G. CHISHOLM.

IV.

TARIFFS, AND INTERNATIONAL COMMERCE.

By J. SHIELD NICHOLSON,

Professor of Political Economy in the University of Edinburgh.

" TO expect," wrote Adam Smith, "that the freedom of trade should ever be entirely restored in Great Britain is as absurd as to expect that an Oceana or Utopia should ever be established in it. Not only the prejudices of the public, but, what is much more unconquerable, the private interests of many individuals, irresistibly oppose it." * This curious example of the danger of political prophecy should suffice to dispel the apathy generally displayed towards any consideration of the fiscal aspects of Britannic Confederation. It is surely absurd, in the light of the history of the United Kingdom during the present century, to put aside proposals for a closer commercial union with the Colonies and Dependencies on the ground either of the prejudices of the public or of the private interests of individuals. Yet nothing is more common than to speak of the complicated tariffs and the vested interests of the newest Colonies as insuperable obstacles to any general fiscal reform. As a matter of historical fact, however, in much less than a century the commercial policy of the British Empire has passed, speaking broadly, from the extreme of central regulation to the extreme of noninterference, and there is, *primâ facie*, no reason why

* "Wealth of Nations," bk. iv. chap. ii. p. 207, M'Culloch's edition.

a reaction should not occur if such a course is shown to be to the mutual advantage of the Colonies and the mother-country.

The Declaration of American Independence and the publication of the " Wealth of Nations " were by far the most important events of the year 1776. Up to this time the monopoly of the Colonial trade was regarded as one of the principal engines of the mercantile system. Most of the great wars of the 18th century, as Professor Seeley * (following Adam Smith) has so well shown, originated in a struggle for trade-supremacy in new countries—and trade-supremacy really meant monopoly. The British Colonies, which were allowed comparatively the greatest freedom, were still placed under very stringent regulations both as regards their exports and imports.† Certain Colonial commodities were *enumerated* in various Acts of Parliament, and could only be exported to the home-country, whilst even non-enumerated products were subject to restrictions of various kinds. But the height of regulation and monopoly was reached in the case of manufactures. " The more advanced or more refined manufactures even of the Colony produce, the merchants and manufacturers of Great Britain choose to reserve to themselves, and have prevailed upon the legislature to prevent their establishment in the Colonies sometimes by high duties and sometimes by absolute prohibitions." ‡ To enforce this policy many curious restrictions were imposed upon the internal commerce of the Colonies.§

* " Expansion of England."
† " Wealth of Nations," bk. iv. chap. vii.
‡ Ibid., p. 261.
§ The following is an example :—" While Great Britain encourages in America the manufacture of pig and bar iron by ex-

Nor was the regulation of trade, strange as it may seem, considered by the Colonists as beyond the legitimate right of the mother-country. The American revolt was not caused by the old-established restrictive policy, nor by any particular modification of an exceptional kind, but was due to an attempt on the part of the British Parliament to collect *revenue* for Imperial purposes without at the same time granting representation. No doubt, in the natural order of development, the old restrictions on Colonial trade would have been modified, and with the adoption of Free Trade by the United Kingdom the same system would naturally have been extended to the Colonies; but it is extremely improbable that, but for the American separation, such a complete reversal of policy could have taken place as to allow the Colonies to impose protective duties on the manufactures of the mother-country. The truth appears to be that American independence completely unnerved British statesmanship in respect to Colonial policy from a commercial and fiscal point of view. For half a century the remnants of the old Colonies, and those

empting them from duties to which the like commodities are subject when imported from any other country, she imposes an absolute prohibition upon the erection of steel furnaces and slit-mills on any of her American plantations. She would not suffer her Colonists to work in those more refined manufactures even for their own consumption. . . . She prohibits the exportation from one province to another by water, and even the carriage by land upon horseback or in a cart, of hats, and of wools and of woollen goods, the produce of America; a regulation which effectively prevents the establishment of any manufactures of such commodities for distant sale, and confines the industry of her Colonies in this way to such coarse and household manufactures as a private family make for its own use, or for that of some of its neighbours in the same province."— "Wealth of Nations," p. 261.

G

subsequently acquired by conquest, were governed from, rather than by, this country through despotic governors and powerless councils; but so soon as the growing strength of the Colonies and the abuses of the Colonial Office made them demand "responsible government," they obtained forthwith practical independence. Just at the very time when this country was abolishing the Corn Laws and preparing the way for general Free Trade, her own Colonies were granted the opportunity of adopting protection, and whilst we have been reducing and simplifying, the Colonies have been extending and complicating, the list of customs-duties. At the same time a specious justification of this timid inactivity was found in the easy popular dogmatism which passed current for an epitome of the "Wealth of Nations." Adam Smith, who had pronounced the Navigation Laws the wisest of all the commercial regulations of England—"dictated by the most deliberate wisdom"—was supposed to have shown once for all that the only duty of the statesman, as regards things in general and Colonies in particular, was to do nothing. The following passage from the "Wealth of Nations"* has been strangely distorted and cramped into the assertion that every Colony should be allowed complete independence :—"To propose that Great Britain should voluntarily give up all authority over her Colonies, and leave them to elect their own magistrates, to enact their own laws, and to make peace and war as they might think proper, would be to propose such a measure as *never was and never will be* adopted by any nation in the World. . . . The most visionary enthusiast would be scarce capable of proposing such a measure with any

* "Wealth of Nations," p. 277.

serious hopes at least of its being adopted. *If* it was adopted, however, Great Britain would not only be immediately freed from the whole annual expense of the peace establishment of the Colonies, *but might settle with them such a treaty of commerce as would effectually secure to her a Free Trade* more advantageous to the great body of the people, though less so to the merchants, than the monopoly which she at present enjoys. By thus parting good friends the natural affection of the Colonies to the mother-country, which perhaps our late (1776) dissensions have well-nigh extinguished, would quickly revive. It might dispose them not only to respect for whole centuries together that treaty of commerce which they had concluded with us at parting, but to favour us in war as well as in trade." Practically what we have done in the last half-century is to give up "all authority" without any attempt to secure the "treaty of commerce." And the curious thing is that the paternity of this policy should be ascribed to Adam Smith.

As a matter of fact this same Adam Smith propounded the most definite and most practicable scheme ever yet published of Imperial Federation. He was not afraid of substituting for the British Parliament the States-General of the British Empire.* "There is not the least probability that the British constitution would be hurt by the union of Great Britain with the Colonies. That constitution, on the contrary, would be completed by it and seems to be imperfect without it. The assembly which deliberates and decides concerning the affairs of every part of the Empire, in order to be properly informed ought certainly to have

* " Wealth of Nations," p. 425.

representatives from every part of it. That this union, however, could be easily effectuated, or that difficulties and great difficulties might not occur in the execution, I do not pretend. I have yet heard of none, however, which appears insurmountable." * Not content with a statement of general principles, Adam Smith actually examined the system of taxation in force at the time in Great Britain, especially the customs, excise, the land-tax, and stamp-duties, with the view of determining how far they might be applicable to all the different provinces of the Empire; and he devised a scheme, according to which " the British Empire would afford within itself an immense internal market for every part of the produce of all its different provinces." †

It is of the utmost importance to observe that the question of tariffs embraces much more than protective duties and Free Trade (in the narrow sense of the terms). Trade may be cramped and petty jealousies may be created by taxes which are imposed avowedly for revenue only. A system of taxation may be thoroughly bad without a single differential duty. The great merit of Adam Smith as a financial reformer — or rather as the teacher of a succession of financial reformers—consisted, not in his mere condemnation of protectionism pure and simple, but in his substitution of a few broad principles of finance in place of an unintelligible mass of historical survivals. If British statesmen had applied these principles as they were generally adopted by the United Kingdom to the rest of the Empire, Adam Smith's Utopia of an immense internal market would have been already realised.

* " Wealth of Nations," p. 281.   † Ibid., p. 425.

The consequence of the want of central control has been vividly presented in the admirable synopsis of the tariffs and trade of the British Empire by Sir Rawson Rawson, which reveals "the inexplicable and purposeless differences in the articles selected for duties and in the rates charged upon them in many parts of the Empire." It is not to be wondered at that the process of compilation should have filled the mind of the compiler with dismay, and that he should write of the "few enthusiasts" who have dreamed of or longed for a common British tariff. But *testimonia non numeranda sed ponderanda sunt*, and one of the "few enthusiasts" is Adam Smith, who has foreshadowed most of the other economic reforms actually accomplished in the present century.

Encouragement may also be found in the fact that the present synopsis is to the corresponding synopsis of the United Kingdom, which confronted Adam Smith, as an unweeded garden to an untouched jungle. Every one knows Sydney Smith's description early in the century of the taxed Englishman, taxed on every article that he used from the cradle to the tomb ; compared with him the most taxed of Colonists bears an easy load.

The main object of the present paper is to point out the principles and the advantages of the financial reforms of the present century in the United Kingdom, with the view of showing that—at any rate to a great extent—similar reforms might be carried out for the rest of the Empire. The question will be considered *first* from the point of view of Revenue (with the indirect consequences), and *secondly* from the point of view of Protection. The first and more important question has too often been neglected in favour of the second, and an attempt may well be made to restore the due balance of emphasis.

"It has been the opinion of many people" (Adam Smith probably had in view his friends the French economists) "that by proper management the duties of customs might, without any loss to the public revenue and with great advantage to foreign trade, be confined to a few articles only." * This has been the guiding principle of British financial reform for a century, and has completely revolutionised our system of taxation. So early as 1787, "to obviate the trouble and inconvenience arising from the multiplicity of Acts relating to the customs, Mr. Pitt introduced a bill for their consolidation," † and there is little doubt that, but for the gigantic wars in which the country was engaged, he would have gone much further in the simplification of the tariff. "No, we must stand till you are seated, for we are your scholars," is the saying attributed to Pitt when Adam Smith came in very late to a distinguished dinner party; and from Pitt to Gladstone all the great British financiers have been scholars of the Scottish Professor. As is usual with British institutions, growth took the place of revolution. The system of natural liberty was not applied like dynamite *à la Française*, but little by little like leaven was introduced until the whole lump was leavened. This style of argument may seem of the nature of ancient history, but it is not so—it is the keystone of Commercial Federation. Let the people of the mother-country and the provinces only remember that the tariffs of the United Kingdom itself, even fifty

* "Wealth of Nations," p. 339.   † Ibid., p. 221, *note.*

years ago, were in a worse confusion than those of the Empire at present, and that a century ago the confusion was infinitely more confounded, and we should hear a good deal less of that "idea of impossibility" which, as Bacon said, is the greatest obstacle to any reform of any kind.

To return to the guiding principle. It is maintained that, so far as revenue from customs-duties is concerned, the provinces might with advantage tax few articles instead of many. It is hardly necessary to add that the smaller the number the greater scope there is for uniformity, and that every reduction brings us nearer fiscal consolidation. It is not easy to give the general reader an adequate notion of the confusion of the present system —he must refer to Sir Rawson Rawson's tables for a complete purview. Samples of chaos are rather curious than instructive, but even samples are better than purely general description. Take the case of *Live Animals :* * In twenty tariffs they are all free, in eleven they are partially free. They are usually charged with specific duties, but in two instances they are charged *ad valorem* as unenumerated articles ; in four some kinds are charged specific rates and others *ad valorem* rates ; and in only five are all kinds charged specific rates. In one of them (the Bahamas) swine are charged by weight 2s. 9½d. per cwt. It is worth remarking that during the first part of this century live animals were on the British tariff list, but in spite of the strength of the landed interest they were taken off. To proceed : "The only article under the head of *Raw Materials* which is almost universally free is manures—guano and chemicals," and the

* " Synopsis of Tariffs," p. 15.

latter, we are reminded in a note, are not strictly raw material. Guano is an excellent beginning of freedom, but why should most tariffs include resin, tallow, tar, and timber? Timber, by the way, since a famous speech by Mr. Gladstone, is the classical example of the advantage of the reduction and final abolition of a customs-duty; as the duty (in this country) was increased the revenue fell, as the duty was lowered the revenue increased, and when at last the duty ended the indirect effects were soon proved to be productive of still greater revenue through the general increase of wealth.

Some Colonies in regard to *manufactures* tax everything not specially enumerated as free, whilst others make a list of one or two hundred for taxation, and leave the rest free. A similar variety of treatment is accorded to *minerals* and *metals*. Coals are free in 23 tariffs. In 11 they are charged specific duties, and in 8 *ad valorem*. Salt is free in 13, it is charged specific duties in 21, and *ad valorem* duties in 8. Will any one seriously maintain that special circumstances, whether of climate, race, history, or prejudice, can justify such a curious diversity of principles and methods? Can any one give a rational answer to the question, why *guano* and *books* should be almost universally free, but almost everything else liable somewhere or other to be hit with a tax? Guano is economically the simplest of raw materials, whilst books are the most complicated of manufactures. Any one who imagines that he has found an answer to this problem may go on to the question, why prints and engravings are generally liable to the unenumerated rate?

It may be said, with much appearance of justice, that uniformity, in itself, has no real advantage, and that our income-tax is itself a congeries of indefensible anomalies.* Certainly no one acquainted with the elements of economic or constitutional history will lay any stress on uniformity, as such; but the point is that these tariffs furnish varieties, not of good, but of bad, principles. From the nature of things a great mass of the articles taxed cannot pay the expense of collection, as was certainly the case with the 1000 articles on the tariff of the United Kingdom some fifty years ago. Government does not gain what the people lose. In this connection it must be noted that the cost of customs-duties is far greater than appears at first sight. In the United Kingdom, under the present simple system, it has been computed (by Jevons, Cliffe Leslie, and others) that the real cost, direct and indirect, of customs- and excise-duties is nearer thirty than the nominal three per cent. of the revenue collected.

There are perhaps only two general arguments which can be advanced in favour of customs-duties of a heavy

* Compare Mr. Gladstone's Financial Statement, April 18, 1853. The income-tax was first imposed as a war-tax, by Pitt, and " dropped along with the purpose of the income-tax in 1816." But it was destined to be revived, and in 1842 Sir Robert Peel "called forth from repose this giant, who had once shielded us in war, to come and assist our industrial toils in peace. . . . It has been the instrument by which you have introduced, and by which ere long I hope you may perfect the reform, the effective reform, of your fiscal and commercial system ; and I for one am bold enough to hope and to expect that in reforming your own fiscal and commercial system, you have laid the foundations of similar reforms—slow, perhaps, but certain in their progress—through every country of the civilised World." Yet, Mr. Gladstone added that, in his opinion, the income-tax was not well adapted for a permanent portion of our ordinary financial system, and he proposed a plan for its abolition, which was to come into effect in 1860.

and extensive kind. In *the first place*, the convenience
to the consumer may be set against the inconvenience
to the trader; and *secondly*, they may be supposed to
encourage native industry. As at present we are only
concerned with revenue-taxes, the argument of convenience must be considered first. Now, it is no doubt
perfectly true that, when a tax is imposed upon some
article of general consumption, the tax-payer does not
notice the little instalments of which his contribution
is made up so much as he does when subjected in some
form or other to the "odious visits" of the tax-gatherer.
This is especially true when the tax is an old tax, for it
is then considered as part of the natural cost of production or of acquisition. "An old tax is no tax" is so far
at least a true saying. Probably not one man in ten
thousand, as he drinks a glass of beer, could tell how
much of the cost was due to taxation; whilst the whole
ten thousand regard the income-tax and various rates as
mulcting them directly in so much money for which
apparently there is no return. Direct taxes savour of
compulsion, whilst indirect taxes are always accompanied
by the pleasures of consumption.

At the same time, however, it is easy to exaggerate
this element of convenience and this apathetic ignorance of the tax-payer. The consumer loves cheapness
and abundance, as was well illustrated recently in the
reaction against the M'Kinley Tariff. It is safe to say
that no argument founded on convenience would induce
the people of this country to submit again to a tax
upon bread. Even the shilling registration-duty was
forced to follow the rest of the Corn Laws. Colonies
which desire to encourage immigration must know very
well that the people whom they wish to attract always

try to form some idea of the scale of living. Because colonies are young nations, it does not follow that colonists are young children, and ought to be treated as such. Colonists above all people are robust and fitted to bear present inconveniences for future advantages. Colonial statesmen who wish to spend extravagantly may find indirect taxation highly convenient; but convenience of this kind is not generally to the interest of the public.

The argument founded on convenience to the tax-payer in his contribution to the revenue obviously loses all significance, or rather may be advanced on its opposite side, when the duties are practically unremunerative; and this must generally happen when the tariff-list is very extensive. By a very natural process taxation on commodities tends to spread from one thing to another—and this for several reasons. There is an idea, which to some extent is well founded, that if taxation is spread over a large surface it will be less felt, and that the yield will also be larger and more stable. British statesmen have several times called attention, with an appearance of apprehension, to the small number of our sources of revenue. Mr. Lowe was induced thereby to invent the Match-Tax, with its elegant motto, "*Ex luce lucellum*"; and Mr. Goschen's Wheel-Tax had doubtless a similar origin, and deserves for its epitaph, "*E vectura vectigal.*"

If one article is taxed, all possible substitutes must be taxed also. If we consider that there are many modes of supplying most wants, and that material things like natural species run into one another, the logical outcome of this principle of taxing substitutes is to tax everything. Certainly the tariff-list tends to become longer at a rapidly increasing rate. Then there is a kind of popular idea of justice which demands that, if the consumption of one class is taxed, other classes shall be taxed in like manner. Thus, in the end, the idea of convenience is lost sight of, and in the vast majority of cases customs-duties are levied, not simply for revenue, but at the best as supports and protectives for other taxes which do yield revenue.

It must be observed, however, at this point, that probably no practical politician would seriously propose to abolish customs-duties altogether.* In the United Kingdom about 22 per cent. of the general revenue is due to that source; but then there are practically (making allowance for substitutes and varieties) only four or five articles on the tariff. The principal reform advocated is an approximation to this simplicity by the Colonies, especially in the abolition of their general taxes on unenumerated articles, and—where enumeration means taxation—in the curtailment of the list. In Tasmania, for example, 10 per cent. is charged on 155 articles, besides other rates on 30 more articles; whilst in Newfoundland and Canada 20 per cent. is levied on unenumerated articles, and enumerated articles pay *ad valorem* rates of 5 to 50 per cent. It is plain, from simple arithmetical principles, that, for the purposes of revenue, such duties are too numerous and too high.

Before passing altogether from the question of the convenience of revenue-duties, some attention must be given to a specious popular argument which will also

---

* Cliffe Leslie, in an essay on Financial Reform, published by the Cobden Club, proposed the abolition of all indirect taxation, but few other reformers have gone beyond the " free breakfast table."

serve as a transition to the question of Protection and retaliation. With many people customs-duties find favour above all other modes of taxation, because they fondly imagine that such taxes are paid by the foreign producer or trader, or in some way by the foreigner in general.

It is a curious illustration of the original sin of all taxation, that the idea of taxing the foreigner, instead of appearing contemptible, as it ought to do, and at any rate unworthy of a great nation, seems to have a peculiar attractiveness both for people and statesmen. It is apparently a survival of the time when, in all languages, the words for stranger and enemy were identical. It is worth recalling some instances of the manifestation of this robust barbarism in British history in former times. Probably the earliest form of taxing the foreigner was by levying tolls on passing bridges, entering markets, &c., and the first Free Traders were merchants who obtained from the king (for a consideration) licences of free passage through his dominions. The much-vaunted clause in Magna Charta, which apparently gave Free Trade to all merchants "saving the ancient customs of the realm," was really intended to secure the rights of the towns and lords of manors in the exaction of dues. Next to tolls were import-duties. These at first took the form of the exaction for the use of the king of a certain proportion of certain things, the levy being at first made in kind. Like other proportional payments, however, they gradually were converted into money, and also became fixed. Thus, the origin of the "ancient and great customs" is to be found in the right of the king to tax the foreigner. The same leading idea is found in the case

of export-duties. For a long period our principal
exports were wool and other raw produce, and the
king was entitled to a certain proportion. In process
of time this proportion gave place to money payments,
and to facilitate and ensure the collection of this revenue
the export of these "staples" was confined to "staple"
towns. These towns were in foreign countries, so that
the foreigner was not only taxed but actually taxed
in foreign parts. It is hardly necessary to recall the
barbaric customs as regards shipwrecks, the piratical
exploits in the Spanish Main, the Navigation Laws,
"really founded," as Adam Smith says, "on national
animosity," and the long list of differential commercial
treaties, to illustrate further the position that for
centuries the idea of taxing the foreigner, directly or
indirectly, was considered in the highest degree laud-
able. It is by no means easy to uproot the sentiments
and prejudices that have grown up with the national
life, and it is very doubtful if "good-will" to the
foreigner, and "peace on earth" were more than pious
war-cries in the battle of Free Trade. If any British
statesman, even at the present time, could formulate a
practicable scheme by which other nations were compelled or induced to pay the principal part of our taxes,
that statesman would be the most popular man in the
country.

Fortunately, however, for the interests of peace and
the development of international trade, taxing the
foreigner is very like "shearing the wolf." It is quite
true that, *theoretically*, under certain conditions, one
nation might obtain from other nations, either by ex-
port- or by import-duties, a considerable part of its
revenue, but it is equally true that these conditions are

extremely unlikely to arise; and, even if they did arise, it is still more unlikely that the wisdom of statesmen would be equal to the task of taking advantage of them. It is important to observe that theoretical exceptions may be admitted whilst the practical application is denied, for no greater harm has been done to the spread of "Free Trade principles," in the broad sense of the term, than by the attempt to reduce them to a fictitious simplicity. To assert that every import-duty must *necessarily* fall on the home consumer is as false as to assert that every export-duty must necessarily fall on the foreign consumer; it is equally untrue to say that *necessarily* the import-duties fall on the foreign producer and the export-duties on the home producer. As a matter of fact the incidence of export- and import-duties, especially when the indirect effects are considered, is the most complicated and difficult problem in economics. It is so difficult, indeed, that one of the strongest arguments in favour of a very simple system of customs-duties is to be found in the uncertain and indeterminate effects to which, especially indirectly, all taxes on commodities give rise.

It is impossible, in a paper of these dimensions, to discuss the theory fully, but sufficient may be said to demonstrate the position that, *primâ facie*, the incidence of import-duties is indeterminate, and that the effects are very wide-reaching. Suppose, then, that a nation suddenly imposes an import-duty upon some important article of commerce. The immediate effect is to raise the price of the article: that is to say, the importers and the foreign producers endeavour to go on with their trade without any loss of profit. But the natural effect of this initial rise in price is to check the demand. The degree of the check, however, depends on the kind of article. It is conceivable that, if the demand is very "inelastic"—if the article, for example, is a necessary, the quantity of which consumed may be regarded as a first charge upon the national income—the rise in price may have very little effect upon the quantity demanded. In this case it is possible that the whole tax would be paid by the home consumer. But suppose, as is possible, that the demand falls off, the question arises : Will the competition of foreigners induce them to lower their prices in order to get the same market as before for their wares ? In this case, again, it is possible that the market of the taxing country is so important relatively to other markets that the foreigners cannot better themselves elsewhere, and to find an entrance must themselves pay the tax—at any rate in the first instance. Between these two extremes any degree of division is *theoretically* possible. We have to consider the intensity of the home demand, the demand of other nations, and the possibility of the use of substitutes of various kinds. The tax may kill the trade altogether, or directly and immediately, so far as demand is concerned, it may have very little effect. For a time at any rate, in the former case, the foreign trader may sell his stock at a loss, and in the latter the consumer may disregard the rise in price.

But demand is only one side of the problem ; for the complete solution we must look at the conditions of supply. If the home consumer bears the whole tax the conditions of supply will of course be unaffected; but if there is any check to demand, and some part of the tax, in the first place at least, falls on the foreigner, it is most important to consider what will be the effect

upon his production. And here arises the question :
Who is the foreigner who is called upon to suffer by
the tax ?   In other words, will the tax in the first place
fall upon the profits, or the wages, or the rents earned
by the particular industry ?   Can the loss in the profit
of the merchant be transferred to the manufacturer or
producer ?   Can he in turn indemnify himself by trans-
ferring the loss to wages, or, in the case of raw produce,
to rent ?   Finally, in any case can the particular class
injured by the tax eventually transfer this loss to the
foreign community in general ?   Now, a little reflection
will show that there is no general answer * to these
questions, but that the particular answer must depend
upon the particular conditions, as, for example, the
mobility of labour and capital in the industry concerned,
the total or partial monopoly of the product, and the
scope for the expansion of industry in other directions.

So far, however, only comparatively immediate effects
of the particular tax have been considered. There are
also important ulterior effects resulting from the fact
that all trade is reciprocal and inter-dependent. If
by taxation importation is crippled, in some branch or
other the export trade must be similarly affected. If,
to take an extreme case, the United States were to prohibit all importation of foreign wares, it is plain that
exportation must also cease. No country would export
without a return ; in trade nothing is given for nothing.
And what is true of the extreme is true in a less degree
of the less extreme. If you check imports, *ipso facto*
you check exports. But then, as soon as exports begin

* The recent reports on the immediate effects of the M'Kinley
Act upon various German exports show that, whilst some have
suffered severely, others have hardly been affected.

to suffer, a similar series of questions arises as to the distribution of the loss. Suppose, for instance, that the general effect of the M'Kinley Act is not to prohibit absolutely but simply to check importation into the United States. The foreigner will suffer, but in what manner and in what degree? Exportation from the States must also be diminished, and American producers will suffer; but, again, in what manner and in what degree? Which will suffer most—the American* or the foreigner? The number of these questions might be indefinitely extended, and the only answer is that an answer is impossible.

At the same time, however, it is possible to indicate in a general way some important practical results, which are confirmed by historical or actual conditions. The first and most obvious is that every tax upon commodities is so far a barrier to trade; it is with manufactures like an increase in the cost of production, with raw materials like an impoverishment of natural resources or deterioration of climate. In whatever way the loss is distributed trade must be injured. There can be no doubt that the heavy duties imposed upon British goods by foreign nations not only affect the foreign consumer but indirectly at least the British people. "Take care of the imports, and the exports will take care of themselves," is a proposition that may easily be turned round, and we may ask: "If the World were to refuse our exports, how should we obtain our imports?" But every foreign customs-duty is a partial refusal.

As regards the primary incidence of import-duties, although theoretically it is indeterminate, there can be little doubt that, as a rule, these duties raise the price of the article to the home consumer. This arises from the fact that there are very few monopolies in foreign trade, and that unless the home consumer pays the greater part of the tax importation will cease. And here it must be observed that, by well-known principles, the article rises in price by more than the amount of the tax. It is clear, for example, that unless the tax is collected immediately before the article goes into the hands of the consumer the burden is cumulative. Merchants must have trade profits upon advances made for taxation, and these profits must include insurance against risk. This loss may be partially mitigated, but can never be wholly neutralised, by bonded warehouses and similar devices; but the broad fact remains that practically, as a rule, indirect taxes take more from the people than they furnish to the Treasury.*

The great evil of indirect taxation is to be found in the indirect effects. It ought not to be necessary to reiterate arguments which British economists have expounded over and over again, and enlightened with a wealth of illustration.† Unfortunately, however, there

---

* "Therefore, for every penny of duty we ask you to surrender, we feel that we are giving nearly double that advantage to the consumer, and a great impetus to trade."—Mr. Gladstone on the *Soap Tax* in Financial Statement, 1853. He went on to show that one indirect effect would be to diminish African slavery, by encouraging the export of palm-oil, and thus the spread of legitimate commerce.

† "The statesman who should attempt to direct private people in what manner they ought to employ their capital would not only load himself with a most unnecessary attention, but assume an authority which could safely be trusted not only to no single person, but to no council or senate whatever, and which would nowhere be so dangerous as in the hands of a man who had folly and presumption enough to fancy himself fit to exercise it."—"Wealth of Nations," p. 200.

is a tendency to believe that truths lose in force as they lose in novelty, and well-established maxims have often been driven out temporarily by re-discovered errors. The two young gentlemen who, according to Swift's diary, " discovered that there is no God," were probably wrong in their reasons ; and in the affairs of the World also wisdom is slowly accumulated. Let the sceptical reader refer to Mr. Dowell's excellent volumes on the history of taxation ; and if any one thinks the incidence of taxes an easy matter, let him look up his Mill (bk. v. chap. iv.).

Another point of practical importance arises in connection with the fallibility of statesmanship. Industrial conditions are constantly changing, and to adjust complicated tariffs to complicated changes is well-nigh impossible.* It is one thing to make out a hypothetical case on paper, and quite another to put it into practice. It is a remarkable fact that the very part of the old protective system which received praise from Adam Smith—namely, the Navigation Laws—was the first part to be attacked by practical Free Traders. The simple reason was that other nations retaliated, and that attempts were then made to arrange reciprocity treaties until such an entanglement of interests and jealousies was created that the whole sytem fell to the ground. Similarly, it is safe to predict that if any general system of customs-duties is to be established for the whole Empire, it must be on broad, simple principles. To suppose that a concession or restriction in one part must be met by some reciprocal operation in another, and that masses of local prejudice must be conciliated

* " Synopsis of Tariffs," p. 16.

in different ways, is to confess that commercial and fiscal union is impossible. Fortunately, however, there can be little doubt that in the provinces as in the centre simplicity would be more productive of revenue than the present complexity.

Hitherto the question has been treated, as far as possible, simply from the point of view of revenue; but to many people the question of revenue seems of far less importance than that of Free Trade and protection. What they demand is not so much Free Trade within the Empire as restriction against the rest of the World, and they apparently assume that this would be the natural development of our present colonial system. Before, then, proceeding to examine briefly the Protectionist ideal, a short passage on the present state of affairs may be quoted from Sir Rawson Rawson. " With regard to the question of duties imposed for the protection of local interests, agricultural or manufacturing, it is not easy to trace them in these tariffs except in two or three prominent cases. It requires local knowledge to determine whether here and there some particular duty has been imposed or incurred for the purpose of encouraging local interests, or whether a generally high rate of duties on manufactures has been imposed for fiscal or for protective purposes. In general the method of favouring such interests has been by abolishing or remitting the duties on articles required for their use— as, for instance, the admission free of duty into several of the West Indian Islands of machinery used in the preparation of Colonial products. . . . The three decided exceptions appear to be Malta, Victoria, and Canada, to which must now be added South Australia." Again, the first sentence in the summary of results runs :—" As it is clear that the duties, with few exceptions, have been imposed mainly for fiscal purposes . . ."

Even if the present state of affairs in the Empire at large were far more protectionist than appears to be the case, it would be superfluous to enter into any general discussion of the principles of Free Trade. For any action must depend, not only on principles, but upon facts and actual conditions. As regards principles, the advocates of Free Trade have unquestionably damaged their cause by dogmatism and exaggeration. By attempting to prove a universal negative—that in no circumstances whatever could a State gain by retaliation or differential duties or other devices of protectionism—they have made their opponents believe that the general case for Free Trade is destroyed if one particular exception can be proved. But, theoretically, as economists of the first rank, from Adam Smith* and Ricardo to Professors Sidgwick and Marshall, have admitted, it is easy to point out, not one, but several exceptions. For practical purposes, however, so far as the British Empire is concerned, these exceptions are simply part of the casuistry of economics; they are like the discussions by moral philosophers of the justification of occasional mendacity. Free Trade, like honesty, still remains the best policy. And it remains the best policy not only because any other policy to be equally successful would require the perfectly wise despot, but largely also, no doubt, because its principles, as applied to ordinary cases, are generally sound. To couple Free Trade within

---

* Adam Smith's four exceptions are well known. "Wealth of Nations," bk. iv. chap. ii. Compare also Sidgwick's "Principles of Political Economy," bk. iii. chap. v.; Marshall's "Principles of Economics," bk. x. chap. xii.

the Empire with Protection against the rest of the
World is to destroy a practical proposal by the addition of a proposal utterly impracticable. This has been
abundantly proved, implicitly if not explicitly, in the
preceding paper of this series by Mr. Chisholm. Is the
United Kingdom likely to tax raw materials such as
cotton and wool, or food-products such as wheat and
mutton, simply with the hope that a policy of this kind
would please the rest of the Empire, or, rather, certain
portions of it? Would the Colonies consent to send all
their produce to our markets and so deprive themselves
of foreign wares? A glance at the facts showing the
magnitude of the foreign trade of the Empire is enough
to prove that the ideal—even if otherwise attractive—
is impossible. A petty uniform duty on all foreign
products would simply be a source of irritation, and is
not worth considering.

The objector may, of course, refer to the policy of the
United States, and may argue that the British Empire
might with advantage follow the same lines of development. But the conditions are wholly different. The
foreign trade of the United States is comparatively
unimportant, whilst that of the United Kingdom is,
with its increasing population, essential to its existence.
And even as regards the United States it is doubtful
if it can long retain its commercial independence; and
its present system is due much more to accident than
design.* It furnishes also a warning, on a colossal
scale, of the principal evil connected with Protection—
namely, the difficulty of getting rid of vested interests,

* See an admirable paper by Professor Taussig, in the *Economic
Journal* for June 1891, on "The M'Kinley Tariff Act."

and the tendency of one protective duty to beget a multitude. Even Adam Smith admitted that "when particular manufactures by means of high duties or prohibitions upon all foreign goods which can come into competition with them, have been so far extended as to employ a multitude of hands, humanity may in this case require that the freedom of trade should be restored only by slow gradations and with a good deal of reserve and circumspection." * But this is surely the strongest argument against the creation by new countries of barriers which, when conditions have changed, it will be so difficult to remove. *Occurrite morbo* should be the motto for those of our Colonies which have to some extent yielded to Protection : the old country is far too seasoned to be inoculated.† Those who advocate any reform must remember that the most fatal obstacle is the exaggerated emphasis laid upon the difficulty of making any change. Get rid of the "idea of impossi-

---

* Book iv. chap. ii.

† A striking instance is given by M'Culloch (Edit. of "Wealth of Nations," note xxv.) of the evil effects of forcing a colonial trade : —"The trade with Canada may be referred to in proof of what has now been stated. It employed a large number of ships and seamen, and seemed to a superficial observer to be highly valuable. In truth and reality, however, it was very much the reverse. A half of this trade was forced and fictitious, having originated in the excess duty which was formerly charged on the Baltic and other foreign timber. The high duty on foreign timber tempted the merchants to resort to Canada, New Brunswick, &c., whence they imported an inferior article at a higher price. . . . By refusing to import the timber of the North of Europe, we proportionally limited the power of the Russians, Prussians, Swedes, and Norwegians to buy our manufactured goods ; while by forcing the importation of timber from Canada, we withdrew the attention of the inhabitants from the most profitable employment they could carry on."

bility," and the task is more than half accomplished. There are, it is true, economic laws which cannot be sent to Saturn, as every nation has found to its cost by numberless experiments, but no system of taxation is by nature eternal and immutable. If little by little Colonial statesmen would follow the example set by the great British financiers of this century, and reduce and abolish their duties, it would be easy to establish a fiscal union. Such a union would bind far more closely than a nominal association for defence. It would naturally lead to the creation of other commercial ties, and silently and insensibly would weld together the fragments of our so-called Empire. For it is as true now as it was when Adam Smith wrote that "this empire has hitherto existed in imagination only. It has hitherto been not an empire but the project of an empire, not a gold mine but the project of a gold mine. . . . It is surely now time that our rulers should either realise this golden dream in which they have been indulging themselves, perhaps, as well as other people, or that they should awaken from it themselves. If the project cannot be completed it ought to be given up. If any of the provinces of the British Empire cannot be made to contribute towards the support of the whole Empire, it is surely time that Great Britain should free herself from the expense of defending those provinces in time of war, and of supporting any part of their civil or military establishments in time of peace, and endeavour to accommodate her future views and designs to the real mediocrity of her circumstances." Such is the concluding passage and, for Britons, the culmination of the whole argument of the "Wealth of Nations," a work which, alike in speculative genius, breadth of view, and practical wisdom, stands alone in political literature. We must choose between federation and disintegration ; and, if we wait for the pressure of a great calamity, the warning of history is that the alternative will no longer be offered.

J. SHIELD NICHOLSON.

V.

ALTERNATIVE MEASURES.

By MAURICE H. HERVEY,

Principal of the Illawarra College, New South Wales.

THE word "alternative" presumes a choice between two possible courses, and with communities, as with individuals, such choice is often perplexing. Above all is it essential that the consequences certainly, or probably, destined to ensue from the selection of one or other alternative be clearly set forth and understood. And, as a necessary preliminary, the alternatives themselves must be exactly defined. Now, *quoad* Britannic Confederation, this preliminary cannot be said to have been overcome, inasmuch as no definite plan of federation has, as yet, been successfully advanced. Where doctors disagree, who shall decide? It is easy to preach the doctrine of Federation. It is not difficult to foreshadow the prospective advantages of race-union and the prospective evils of race-disintegration; and this, indeed, is primarily the object of this paper. But of what use proposing alternatives, one of which has not been shown to be possible of adoption?

This is unquestionably the reason why the entire question has so long hung fire. Perhaps no question of modern times has more generally engaged the attention of politicians than the abstract idea of drawing together more closely the ill-defined, relaxed bonds of British race-unity. Our ablest writers have discussed it, our best orators have waxed eloquent over it, an

influential League has for years advocated it, and striven
to keep it prominently before the public mind. And
yet the great cause has made but little real progress.
Neither the Home nor the Colonial public has, in ex-
pressive modern *argot,* "caught on." Federation is as
little generally understood as bi-metallism or the zone
freight system. And this, mainly, because no one
knows exactly what it exactly means, or how it can
possibly be brought about. Thus, while separation from
the mother-country, as one alternative, is an eventuality
realised as possible by all the Colonies, definite federal
union with her, as the other alternative, has hitherto
never assumed a tangible shape capable of serious
discussion.

From a study of the papers upon Britannic Confederation which have already appeared in this Series, it
appears that two of the four distinguished contributors
regard some form of commercial union as an essential
preliminary; one prefers that the initial steps should
take the form of defence; whilst the fourth would
appear to reject the federal idea as wholly inconsistent
with the dignity of Great Britain. Each one of these
proposed ways of viewing the question has a strong
following, the commercial-union plan being, for the
moment, perhaps, most in favour. Moreover, the publi-
cations of the Imperial Federation League reveal the
existence of yet another class of thinkers, who advocate
political union without more ado; whilst in the back-
ground lie the great mass of the British communities
placidly indifferent to the whole affair, quite content to
"leave well alone," satisfied to leave the decision to
Providence and time.

Now, Providence, as we know, helps those who help

themselves. Time is usually a mere witness to the succession of effect upon cause. And the "leave well alone" platform is untenable because, in the first place, things at present are very far from being well; and, secondly, because they give every promise of becoming far worse in the near future.

Yet, how bring these facts home to the popular mind? Probably those only who have been in the habit of addressing mixed audiences can rightly appreciate the general ignorance rife in one British community as to the condition and prospects of other British communities. And nowhere is this more noticeable than in Great Britain. Such audiences love to be told that they have a vested interest in the largest and wealthiest empire of which history furnishes any record; and with maps, diagrams, and clear explanations, it is not difficult to make this clear to all. Upon this ground it is easy to evoke enthusiasm. But when a speaker proceeds to describe how this vast heritage has been gained only at the cost of enormous sacrifices and of ceaseless effort, and that it can only be kept upon the same terms, the enthusiasm dies out. That "property has its duties as well as its rights" is a trite popular saying upon which much modern legislation has been based; but, when the Imperial interests are concerned, it is the hardest of all axioms to drive home. And yet, not until it shall have been driven thoroughly well home, can any strong expression of the national will be looked for. No great movement ever yet came to a successful issue which was not supported by the people. Politicians and philosophers may instruct, admonish, but they must in the end move with the irresistible current of public opinion. So, too, it is easier to convert, to convince a hundred well-informed,

thinking men than one uncultured artisan ; but unless
the artisan be convinced the conversion of the hundred
goes but a very little way.   It is not sufficient to make
it clear to readers of high-class magazines that prompt,
definite action is necessary to save the Empire from
impending disintegration, and that such disintegration
would be an irretrievable national calamity.   The reali-
ties of the situation, the prospects and the perils which
confront further national progress, must be disseminated
throughout every land peopled by men of British race,
by every available channel of popular instruction, and,
notably, by the popular press.   Hitherto this press has
moved but sluggishly in the matter, alleging (and, it
must be confessed, not without good show of plausibility)
that, until the leading prophets of Federation shall have
agreed amongst themselves as to the lines upon which
race-unity should be maintained, no programme can be
submitted for national approval or rejection.   But this
is, in reality, rather an excuse than a reason for shelving
the question.   The prophets are at least agreed in advocating the necessity for federation.   That they are not
also agreed as to ways and means of bringing it about
is mainly owing to the extreme difficulty of estimating
what methods would most commend themselves to the
bulk of English-speaking communities.   It is to be
noticed that the question, albeit the most mighty in
prospective results ever submitted to a nation, is not
one which tangibly affects the conditions of daily life.
The least intelligent members of a community can
appreciate the importance of the cheap loaf, of reduced
taxation, or of extension of the franchise ; and, upon
such questions, the popular voice is wont to speak
promptly and emphatically enough.   But of the British

Empire, its history, its value, its prospects, nine-tenths of the race to which it belongs know extremely little and care less. This indifference (which posterity will so harshly stigmatise) springs from no want of patriotism, of which an ample supply lurks in most British hearts, but from sheer downright ignorance of the issues at stake. And this, the most insuperable of all stumbling-blocks upon the steep path to national unity, the press is, by far, the most potent agency to remove. I, for one, would rather see but a single one of the widely-circulated London "dailies" advocating the good cause with a will than learn that a hundred new branches of the Federation League had sprung into existence.

If it be asked *how* the slumbering lion of public opinion is to be aroused, upon what lines the nation is to be convinced of the necessity for definite action, then the reply would appear to lie in the clear establishment of two single propositions :—

I. The loosely-connected component elements of what is at present vaguely known as the British Empire cannot hold together very much longer under existing conditions; that is, the only alternative to some form of closer union, or federation, is disintegration.

II. Federation would be to the advantage of all British communities, individually and collectively. The alternative, disintegration, would, on the contrary, obviously at once destroy their collective interests, and would not only injure the individual interests, but would, in the case of many communities, jeopardise their very existence.

Of these two propositions, the first appeals with equal force to Great Britain and to the Colonies; the second

I

must be viewed from two standpoints: that of the Englishman living in Great Britain, and that of the Englishman living in one or other of the Colonies.

I. Federation or Disintegration?

When, more than three centuries ago, England first fairly awoke to the pangs of Earth-hunger, she came very late into the field. Spain, Portugal, Holland, and France had all secured a considerable start in the race for empire. But, thanks to her insular position, her gradually established superiority at sea, the generally judicious part she was enabled to take in the successive struggles between Continental nations, and the commercial basis upon which she strengthened her steady advance, she finally emerged with more foreign possessions than she well knew what to do with. Not more than she wanted, be it well understood; because the colonising propensities of Englishmen are apparently insatiable; but certainly more than she could reasonably expect to keep for an indefinite period upon an indefinite plan. As regards India and her other alien-peopled Possessions, her policy has, indeed, been clear and consistent. They were and are conquests, which must be kept by the power of the sword. But, in dealing with the vast territories colonised by communities of British blood, Great Britain's course has been lamentably erratic, equally generous and inconsistent. Whilst bestowing upon mere handfuls of settlers enormous areas of land and ample legislative freedom, thereby engendering the idea of future independent nationality, she has retained in her own hands paramount powers which are, to the Colonial mind, irritatingly suggestive of Colonial inferiority. Complacently recognising the probability that, by-and-by, these communities would sigh for complete independence, she has throughout acted as though they would for ever remain tied to her apron-strings. Potential nationalities, even though youthful, should early be taught to rely mainly upon themselves; but the Colonies have, throughout, been permitted—nay, encouraged, to rely wholly upon the mother-country. They have been treated like spoilt children, and they have sighed for manhood, also, like spoilt children, without realising what the responsibilities of manhood entail. To maintain Imperial fleets and armies, people in the United Kingdom have for years been groaning under a taxation which, owing to their harder conditions of life, they could ill afford to pay; whilst the Colonials, who, owing to the easier conditions of life abroad, could afford to pay their share very well, have (until recently, and then but to a trivial amount) escaped scot-free. So long, indeed, did they enjoy this immunity, that they now view any proposals to tax them, *for their own defence*, as a hardship scarcely to be borne. Had Britain, before signing away her territories with so lavish a hand, insisted upon a fair distribution of the revenue necessary for Imperial purposes over the whole Empire, this unfair protest would never have arisen; for true it is that "an old tax is no tax." Colonials now evince no gratitude for past favours; they stare steadily at the future; and their platform is practically this: "If, in the past, Great Britain has protected us, and lent us money, and built us up generally, she doubtless had her own reasons for doing so and made a good profit out of the transaction. Our great danger from attack at present (whatever it may have been formerly) lies in some outcome of her foreign policy, in which we are not consulted. If we are to protect ourselves—which is the real meaning of paying for our own protection—we must either have a voice in this perilous foreign policy, or cut the Imperial connection, and start a less hazardous foreign policy of our own." And upon the just principle that "they who contribute shall spend," it will be conceded that there is much of force in the Colonial contention. It is, at all events, clear that the present dead-lock cannot endure.

But even upon the not very warrantable assumption that Great Britain, rather than provoke a breach with the Colonies, should waive the question of defence-contributions and continue to bear the burthen alone, the further question arises : Could she maintain the Empire, in its present dislocated condition, for any measurable length of time ? Sharp and swift comes the answer : No. It is useless blinking our eyes to the fact that, with perhaps a single exception, Great Britain is regarded with jealousy or dislike, or both, by the Great Powers of Europe. Yet she must play her part in every fluctuation of the balance of power.

Does the most patriotic of Jingoes seriously believe that, in the event of war, and with a great maritime nation against her, Great Britain could afford protection (with her existing armaments) to her foreign Possessions ? Or that, if her own shores were in danger, she could leave squadrons in the Atlantic or the Pacific ? And what could unprotected Possessions do, save shelter themselves beneath the neutral flag of independence ? Surely the position needs but small argument, beyond a bare glance at the perils which lie ahead. And, equally surely, if Britain and the Colonies neglect to set the Imperial house in order, jointly, and whilst yet there is time, they can look for no other result than that it should fall in ruins about their ears.

There are not wanting those who, in the face of the constantly increasing armaments of Europe, profess a firm conviction that the very magnitude of these war-like preparations will effectually glue the sword to the scabbard until, by common consent, a general disarmament takes place. They point to the fact that, with modern weapons, the struggle would necessarily be so unprecedentedly bloody, that no government would face the responsibility of throwing down the glove. History, neither past nor modern, would seem to justify such sanguine views. But even if we admit, for the sake of argument, that there will be no European war, or that, if there be one, Britain will contrive to steer clear of it, the only difference which this hypothesis can make, so far as Imperial prospects are concerned, is that, in lieu of rapid disintegration consequent upon war, there would supervene more gradual disintegration consequent upon diversity of interests. The great Colonies are now well past the leading-string stage. They possess all the elements necessary towards forming distinct nationalities; and each day their position, as merely dependent factors in the sum-total of Britain's greatness, becomes more irksome to them. They are powerless to make a commercial treaty with even sister-colonies without admitting to its provisions Britain's foreign customers. They cannot even communicate with a foreign nation, except through the British Foreign Office. They labour under all the vexatious disadvantages of vassalage, and they resent it. Canada is, indeed, handicapped by the proximity of the United States, and fears absorption into the giant Republic, did she part company with Britain.   But Australia is not so handicapped, nor is South Africa; and the steps already taken by the former towards the establishment of a "Commonwealth" (the mere name of which is inconsistent with a monarchical form of government) plainly shows that Australian patience is rapidly approaching the vanishing-point.   And the loss of Australia, besides meaning the loss of more than one-third of the whole territory in the Empire, would be a striking precedent for others to follow.   The Australian Colonies cannot fairly be blamed or accused of want of patriotism in the steps they have taken and purpose to continue.   They have waited a long time for some sign from the mother-country.   When the Imperial Federation League came into recognised existence, the Colonies had already held preliminary federal meetings at Hobart Town.   These, failing the concurrence of New South Wales, fell through, or, more correctly, were postponed. But, finding that Imperial Federation fell flat in England, they revived the idea of federating *inter se*, and even New South Wales this time took part in the proceedings.   Of course, all British Colonies realise full well that their position would be far higher as States of a Britannic Confederation than as embryo republics. But failing any authoritative invitation to join such a confederation, they are preparing for the day of British disintegration.   Such, at least, is the conviction which a residence of twelve years in the various Colonies has forced upon the mind of the writer.

Finally, as to the question whether even loss of the Colonies would be equivalent to loss of empire to Great

Britain, I can only say that, in my judgment, it would. An empire, of a sort, she could still have, so long as she could keep a hostile Power out of India, and maintain her rule over her Asiatic subjects at odds of four thousand to one. "If this be empire, make the most of it," —but it is not the sort of empire foreshadowed by a Britannic Confederation.

II. The Profit and Loss of the Alternatives.

This section of the subject may conveniently be resolved into (broadly) two sub-sections: Financial-Commercial and Political. And, moreover, as the considerations involved are not quite identical, so far as native-born and colonial-born Britons are respectively concerned, it would appear advisable to rehearse them separately.

(i.) Financial-Commercial Considerations (*as viewed from Great Britain*).

Most business men, if confronted with the alternatives of continuing a business, or carrying it on, would pause to consider the amount of capital sunk in that business. Englishmen are nothing if not business men. It therefore behoves them, as a preliminary, to total-up the amount already invested in their Empire. What the total *might* be stated at, from first to last, it simply staggers the imagination to conceive. But here are a few items which, as it were, lie upon the surface.

To, say, 100 years' expenses incurred for
defence of the said Empire at the
(very moderate) rate of £25,000,000
per annum £2,500,000,000
To extraordinary war expenses (Crimean
and petty wars, &c.) 350,000,000
National Debt (1815) 850,000,000
Interest paid on National Debt since
1815 . . . . 2.040,000,000
_____

£5,740,000,000

*Five thousand seven hundred and forty millions ster-
ling!* One has to think the figures over for a few
minutes to get an idea of what they really mean. Yet
a few minutes' more reflection will show they are by
no means an exhaustive statement of the sums actually
spent and paid for. Yet stay! the odd £740,000,000 has
not yet been paid for. It is, in fact, still owing, and
is commonly known as the National Debt. By whom
owing? Nominally by Great Britain. But is it conceivable that a Britannic Confederation, once organised,
would consent to saddle the mother-nation with a debt
contracted for the Empire? Impossible. There is
nothing radically mean in the Colonial character: if
anything, it errs on the score of liberality, where once
its sense of honour is touched. To even hint *now* to
the Colonies that they should recognise any liability
in this obligation (to which they owe their very existence), would be ridiculous, because they have no voice
in the government of the Empire which it was expended
to build up. But, offer them a proportionate share,
as co-heirs, in this Empire, and this National Debt
would be transferred to the Britannic Confederation,

without so much as a division. More seriously, and apart from the National Debt, is Great Britain prepared to recognise that the major portion of the huge balance must be written off as a bad debt? At present she still rules paramount over what might easily be made the coming race. This is the consideration, still hers, for the thousands of millions, to say nothing of the blood, expended. Will she allow it, of her own mere supineness, without an effort, without one single motherly call to her own flesh and blood, to pass away from her—for ever?

The taxpayer in the United Kingdom may next proceed to inquire what becomes of the enormous revenue which he is annually called upon to contribute. He will find that considerably more than half (some £50,000,000) is swallowed up in what may fairly be termed Imperial expenses—that is, in army and navy, fortifications, the Diplomatic and Consular Services, &c. About one-quarter goes to cover interest upon the National Debt. The balance, less than one-quarter, remains for purely home expenditure. Is this, in his judgment, a satisfactory state of affairs? He is begged to observe that the Colonial gets just as much out of the fifty millions as he does, and, until recently, paid not one shilling towards the amount (now he contributes towards the wages of the crews of the Australian Squadron). If he travels, he enjoys every privilege of British citizenship, the use of the Consular Service, the protection of the flag; and for these benefits he pays nothing. Nothing can well be clearer than that advantages enjoyed by the whole Empire should be paid for by the whole Empire, and not by a fractional portion of it. But if it be asked why this obviously

fair principle is not carried into effect, the old answer
crops up : Great Britain alone furnishes the revenue
necessary to give effect to and sustain her Imperial
policy, because she alone shapes and directs that policy.
If it be true that they only who contribute should expend, it is, conversely, true that they only who expend
should contribute. The Colonies, having no voice in
Imperial policy or expenditure, fail to see why they
should have any hand in contributing. This is clear.
But it is equally clear that if they *had* a voice in the
Imperial councils, they would necessarily bear their
fair share of the Imperial expenditure.

The public debts of the Empire (apart altogether from
the debt of Great Britain) amount to £540,000,000,
nearly three-fifths of which are represented by Colonial
Government securities, and almost the whole of the
entire sum is due to British investors. Now, so long as
the Colonies remain under the British flag, these securities are rightly deemed to be first-class. But how
would they be regarded did the Colonies blossom
forth as infant republics? And it may be noted
that the English Supreme Court has struck a note of
warning in this connection by persistently refusing to
sanction the investment of trust funds in Colonial
stocks. But were the Colonies definitely admitted as
States of a Britannic Confederation, these same stocks
would permanently rank amongst the very best securities.

Nor must it be forgotten that an enormous amount of
British capital has been invested in Colonial industrial
enterprises. This capital also may be regarded as safe
so long as Great Britain's existing relations with the
Colonies endure. But, once more, how would they be

regarded in the event of these relations undergoing a rupture?

The force of these financial considerations will probably be readily admitted; indeed they are but a few amongst many. Of still greater weight are the considerations suggested by commerce, upon which Britain's very existence may be said to depend. If we examine into the existing conditions of Great Britain's trade we find that, out of a total of £741,000,000, seventy-six millions represent trade with British Possessions (India, &c.) other than British Colonies, one hundred and seven millions with her Colonies, and the balance with the rest of the World. Consequently, the Colonial trade proper represents but one-seventh of the total. And the reflection suggests itself that, even supposing Colonial independence to mean cessation of trade with Great Britain (which it obviously never could mean), the loss, though serious, would be by no means synonymous with commercial ruin. This is a fair argument; but it is furthermore to be borne in mind that the future must be studied. Are these proportions likely to be maintained? It is not conceivable that they should. Considering that the Colonies have, all told, but a population of thirteen millions, the amount of their present trade with Britain is phenomenal—nearly half that of Britain's trade with the United States, which have a population of sixty-two millions, and one-third greater than is furnished by all other British Possessions (including highly-prized India) with their two hundred and eighty millions of Asiatics. If, actually, this handful of Colonials stands forth so prominently, how about the time (and no very long time either) when that handful shall double, treble, quadruple in number?

Or, put it this way—How would a proposal be received in Great Britain involving the loss of the Indian trade, or a _laissez-aller_ policy tending to the loss of that trade? Would it not raise an outcry from John o' Groat's to Land's End? Yet that much-prized, exaggerated Asiatic trade is far below the Colonial trade in value,* and must in the future continue to take a seat still further back,—and this, too, in face of the fact that, whereas the Colonial trade is heavily hampered by Protective tariffs, that of India is almost free. Who can estimate the volume of Colonial trade which would spring up were it made _possible_ for the Colonies to repeal their tariffs? I do not know. But this I know, that so long as independence is the only goal which Colonials can see in sight, they _must_ and will strive, by a Protective policy, to make themselves productively independent of the rest of the World, Great Britain included. Colonials are not simpletons; they are quite capable of appreciating the advantages of Free Trade; but they also realise what their position would be if, relying entirely upon Great Britain for manufactured goods, the mother-country even temporarily lost her command of the seas. They are not so thoroughly convinced as is the typical Jingo of Britain's invincibility, and they do not clearly understand her foreign policy. But a Britannic Confederation, of which they would be factors—well, _that_ might be considered invincible, and, at least, they would have a voice in its policy.

It need scarcely be pointed out, that the continually increasing European and American tariffs are causing the gravest anxiety in commercial circles in Great

* Compare, however, Mr. Chisholm's references to India.—_Ed._

Britain ; indeed, it would seem to be but a question of a very few more years for these tariffs to reach the prohibitive point when commerce must cease. How about Britain's trade then ? The thing is quite possible ; for be it never forgotten that *Great Britain is the only nation in the World absolutely dependent upon commerce.*

A truth will always bear repetition. "Trade follows the flag." We have neither space, nor is there any necessity, here to illustrate the exactness of this time-honoured maxim further than to point out that, if the trade-returns be carefully analysed (and the work is pleasant mental recreation), its truth is verified with surprising precision. And it is natural that it should be so, for what does the flag mean save identity of commercial and national interests which all are alike impelled to assist and maintain.

(ii.) FINANCIAL-COMMERCIAL CONSIDERATIONS (*as viewed from the Colonies*).

Upon the Colonial mind the fact that the mother-country has spent some thousands of millions sterling would make no great impression ; the average settler would take it very much as a young man would take the information from his father that his education and maintenance had cost several thousands up to date—as a matter of course, with the amount of gratitude inspired by individual disposition. He might be brought to see that he morally owes a portion of Great Britain's National Debt ; but that would depend very much upon how the obligation might be placed before him.

As regards contribution towards current Imperial expenses, his attitude is resolute and clear. He recognises the necessity for defence against possible attack, and that such defence costs money. To the Canadian the question is far more simple than to the Australian; and Canada has found it expedient to adopt what is practically a form of conscription as a safeguard against possible attack from the United States. But the Australian has no such towering neighbour, and very much overrates the Imperial connection as his only possible source of danger. If attacked by a foreign power, it could only be, he alleges, because that power would be at war with Britain upon some question to him at once trivial and unintelligible. He, personally, cares not one straw who owns Constantinople, or who dominates Egypt, because his trade with India is but small, and his route does not lie through the Suez Canal. His trade with Britain and with Europe does, but then there is always the alternative Cape route. Yet, he altogether forgets that he would be exposed to at least equal perils were his political connection with Great Britain severed. What guarantee would he have that foreign nations would leave him in undisturbed possession of a vast continent were the protection of Great Britain withdrawn? How would he fare in a war with France or Germany, or even with China?

He realises that his continued progress must largely depend upon his ability to borrow largely and at a cheap rate; but he avers that he can do so, not because he flies the Union-Jack, but because British capitalists are familiar with the vast resources of his Colony, and that they would continue to lend upon the strength of these resources. They have lent freely to corrupt, ill-governed, nondescript South American republics: why not to republics peopled and governed by men of British race?

But here again he overlooks much that is important. There is such a thing as borrowing too dear. The South American States have, for years, been borrowing upon exorbitant terms, have nearly all proved unable to meet even the interest upon their loans, and are hovering upon the brink of bankruptcy. Even supposing that colonies converted into republics could borrow, is it to be supposed that they could borrow at present rates? And, from another point of view, is it conceivable that British capital would flow in to aid industrial enterprises, as it now does, were it being invested in infant republics?

As regards his commerce, the Colonial takes the broad platform that Great Britain would continue to trade as freely with young republics as with dependent Colonies. That, doubtless, is mainly true. But how about that trade if British capital were withdrawn or sparingly and dearly lent? His imports would be rigidly gauged by his exports; and how could the latter be increased or even maintained without help? Let him remember that, as matters stand, British commerce is very far from being mainly dependent upon the Colonies, whereas Colonial trade is most distinctly mainly dependent upon Great Britain. It would be a bad thing for Britain to lose or to cripple her Colonial trade, but it would be more than a bad thing for the Colonies: it would be commercial ruin. Remove the British-owned ocean-going ships from Melbourne or Sydney, and what would remain?

Nay, let the Colonial rather strive to realise that separation from Great Britain would entail stagnation and loss upon a scale which it is pitiful to contemplate. If he be driven to independence, by force of circumstances or by delay, amounting to refusal on the part of Britain to receive him into federation with her, then indeed must the burthen be borne, the loss and the stagnation endured. But, in the meanwhile, let him be somewhat more outspoken as to his willingness to accept Confederation if offered to him, realising that it is not the sort of proposal which a great nation can be expected to make where there is a chance of refusal.

(iii.) POLITICAL CONSIDERATIONS (*viewed from Great Britain*).

Of existing great powers, but one, the United States, can be said to enjoy absolute immunity from attack, unless, indeed, the States themselves deliberately provoke a conflict. They have a vast continuous area, affording sufficient scope for all reasonable national dreams of expansion for many centuries to come. They are ruled by the same laws and speak the same tongue. They come up, as near as may be, to even Professor Freeman's exacting definition of an "ideal nation." Great Britain, whose Empire extends, in a confused sort of way, over three times the area and five times the population, is so far from enjoying similar immunity that she may fairly be described as the most vulnerable of all and the worst prepared to repel attack. Her own shores are rather supposed to be, than known to be, safe: that is, they are still guarded by the power which has maintained them inviolate in the past—a powerful fleet. But her outlying dominions can, by no stretch of imagination, be even supposed to be safe. It would be hard to point out a single one that *is* safe—unless, perhaps, Gibraltar. And this insecurity springs from two causes, the one obvious, the other not quite so self-evident. Geographical situation is, of course, the obvious cause, and, necessarily, a permanent one, to be remedied only by increased speed of communication. The other cause lies in the ill-defined haphazard nature of her tenure of the most important of her Possessions. Of course I allude more particularly to the Colonies; but even India is in the same category.

From time to time the entire patrimony of the British race has been made over in free gift to a few millions of settlers, and these are now practically as much masters of 8,000,000 square miles of territory as Great Britain herself is of the 121,000 square miles contained in the United Kingdom. Of this clear convincing proof was given in the replies returned by the various Colonial Governments to a circular sent to them by a strong committee of both Houses of Parliament asking for grants of land suitable for emigration upon a large scale. These replies were a distinct refusal all round, the clearest explanation whereof was given by Sir Henry Parkes, the Premier of New South Wales, viz., that such a proposal was utterly inconsistent with the Australian watchward, "Australia for the Australians." This, it might be thought, would have exhausted English patience. But not at all; the emigration scheme was dropped, that was all. And, as though to justify the Colonial attitude, within two years of this incident, Great Britain conceded her last remaining million square miles to fifty thousand settlers in Western Australia. It is not, of course, pretended that any of the Colonies have gone the length of closing their ports to would-be immigrants; nay, they encourage what are deemed to be immigrants of the right sort, that is, with money in their pockets, or skilled artisans (in moderate numbers),

K

or domestic female servants (to any extent). But these are precisely the very persons whom the mother-country can least spare.

Now, is it not high time to let it be known to the dominant democrat labour factions in all the Colonies, that neither is Australia for the Australians, nor Canada for the Canadians, nor South Africa for the South Africans, but that all these belong to, and are "for the entire British race"? And how accomplish this so effectually as by re-absorbing these somewhat self-assertive offshoots into a re-organised, federated empire? To deprive them by force of rights already conceded is out of the question. What other alternatives exist, except to allow them to drift off or break off into complete independence?

Perhaps the greatest of all advantages foreshadowed by a perfected federal policy is that, whereas a dislocated empire is a source of weakness, a securely-knit empire would be as a tower of irresistible strength. At present Britain's foreign policy really consists in playing one Great Power off against another, whilst she plays herself off as occasion may appear to offer. She is not powerful enough to hold her Empire in the teeth of the World; she knows it, and they know it. But a Britannic Confederation would be under no necessity to follow any such hide-and-seek tactics. It would from the very outset be quite strong enough to assert itself, and, if need were, to hold its own against anything short of a universal coalition—an eventuality which need hardly be taken into account. Can any reasoning man pretend that Britain would not gain enormously in political power by exchanging her present status, as harassed guardian of a confused string of Possessions, for one where she would figure as Parent and Premier State in a world-wide and powerful Britannic Confederation?

(iv.) POLITICAL CONSIDERATIONS (*viewed from the Colonies*).

It has already been pointed out that the Colonial could not safely, or even securely, rely upon immunity from attack from one of the Great Powers were British protection withdrawn.   But even supposing that, by making concessions and by skilful diplomacy, the Colonies did contrive to secure a peaceful existence, what would their status in the World be?   Each group would necessarily be at the expense of providing and maintaining an army and a fleet, and of organising and paying for a wide-spread Consular Service, just as the impoverished South American Republics have had to do. And what force would their diplomatic utterances carry, say, in Paris or in Berlin?   Or how would Canadian rights in Behring Sea or Australian rights in the Pacific be enforced?   To whom would, or could, the travelling Colonial apply for redress or assistance, say, in Chili or in Persia, or anywhere else?   To his Consul? He might just as well apply to the nearest telegraph-post.   The United States is powerful enough.   Yet, during the Argentine Revolution of July 1890, I have seen the British Consulate at Rosario literally besieged by American citizens begging for *British* safe-conducts. France is powerful enough.   Yet, during the last Chilian civil war, I have seen French subjects arrested and otherwise annoyed (until a French war-ship appeared upon the scene) to an extent which, had they been British subjects, would have brought the guns of H.M.S. *Warspite* to bear upon the *Intendencia* at Valparaiso. Germany is powerful enough. Yet she was fain to beg permission (during the same war) of the British Foreign Office to place her subjects resident in Chili under British protection. Let the Colonial be well assured that there is no such passport throughout the entire World as to be able to declare "I am a British subject." I grant that, as matters now stand, it would not add to his dignity abroad to explain that he was a Canadian or a Queenslander. But the amended form, "a subject of the Britannic Confederation," would very soon be understood as synonymous with *Noli me tangere*. Indeed, from this political point of view, the Colonies have vastly more to gain than even Great Britain herself.

MAURICE H. HERVEY.

VI.

THE CONSOLIDATION OF THE BRITISH EMPIRE.

By LORD THRING, K.C.B.

THE CONSOLIDATION OF THE BRITISH EMPIRE.

A UNITED British Empire, going forth—not con-
quering or to conquer, but to regulate commerce
and spread peace and civilisation throughout its limits,—
would be a dominion of a grandeur and beneficence as
yet unknown among the kingdoms of the World.

The possibility of the establishment of such a reign
of peace and goodwill has been widely canvassed. On
the one side it has been said that the component parts of
the Empire are so divergent in their interests that they
will not admit of being welded into a compact mass.
On the other side, it is replied that, granted that territories such as India and the spheres of influence in
Africa cannot enter into complete union with Canada
and Australia, there still remain a number of Colonies
capable of being moulded into an efficient working
Empire. In short, the solution of the problem of
Britannic Confederation must depend largely on what
is meant by *confederation*—what is the degree of union
indicated, and what territories are intended to be tied
together by a bond of greater or less stringency. The
object of the present article is to deal with the whole
question impartially. The facts, on which the conclu-
sions in it are based, will in the main be found in the

able papers already published in this Series. The task
set before me is to collect and compare the results of
those papers, and to present in a succinct form the
existing conditions of the British Empire, and the
means to be adopted to draw closer the bonds of union,
or at all events to counteract the forces tending to
greater disintegration.

The extent and general characteristics of the British
Empire will be best understood by a careful examination
of the excellent map, specially prepared to illustrate
this series of papers, and appended to this number. It
should be added, that the map was designed by Mr.
Silva White and compiled by Mr. J. G. Bartholomew.
The Empire comprehends about one-fifth of the land-
surface of the globe, and contains a population in the
gross of 348,000,000. The countries of the British
Empire occupied by settlers of European, and principally British, origin are distinguished on the map
from those countries of the Empire in which the native
element is in numerical preponderance. In the following pages the term Colonies is restricted to the former,
whilst the latter are classed under the generic name
of Dependencies. This classification has been adopted,
inasmuch as the main object of this paper is to deal
with cert in typical Colonies rather than to discriminate
accurately between the great variety of governments
prevailing in the British Empire. The other original
features of the map explain themselves. It may, however, be well to draw attention to the fact that an
attempt has been made to show at a glance, by distin-
guishing the places where there are British Ambassadors
or other accredited Diplomatic or Consular agents of
the British Government, the vast organisation main-

tained by Great Britain for the protection and assistance of all the subjects of the Empire.

The United Kingdom, the centre and head of this vast aggregate of nations, has an area of 121,481 square miles, and a population of 38,000,000. The Indian Empire is far the most important of the dark-coloured Dependencies, and has an area of 1,533,611 square miles, containing a population of 286,000,000. The spheres of influence in Africa comprehend an area of about 2,462,000 square miles, with a large population, the amount of which is quite unknown.

The Colonies to be chiefly noted are the Dominion of Canada, Australia, New Zealand, and the Cape. The area and population of each of these Colonies is given below. The remainder of the Empire consists of numerous smaller Colonies; but, for the purpose of this paper, no detailed description is required of their extent or population.

	Area. Square Miles.	Population.
Canada	3,456,383	4,830,897
Australia	2,944,628	3,038,763
Cape Colony	221,311	1,527,224
New Zealand	104,235	668,353
Remainder (excluding India)	649,000	9,000,000
	7,375,557	19,065,237

The greater part of this vast Empire has been acquired during the course of 150 years by settlement, by conquest, and by that most dubious form of acquisition which passes under the name of annexation.

Having now stated the relations between Great Britain and her Colonies in respect to area and population, let us proceed to the consideration of their commercial relations. By the old school of political economists these would have been deemed the only ties worth considering: we now know that sentiment and passion are as powerful, or more powerful, factors in the friendship of nations than even money and trade. Still, as the argument of the purse is a strong one, let us see how that stands between the mother-country and her children. In round numbers,

The Trade of the United Kingdom

With Canada	. .	is $2\frac{3}{4}$ per cent. of her whole trade.
,, Australia	. .	$5\frac{3}{4}$
,, Cape Colony	.	$1\frac{1}{2}$
,, New Zealand	.	$1\frac{3}{4}$
		— $11\frac{3}{4}$ per cent. or not quite $\frac{1}{8}$ of the whole.
,, Remainder	.	$4\frac{3}{4}$
,, India	. .	9
,, Foreign Countries		$74\frac{1}{2}$

From this table it will be seen that, viewed solely from a pecuniary point of view, the trade of the United Kingdom with the Colonies, though of great importance, is far inferior in magnitude to her trade with foreign countries, being less than 12 per cent. of her whole trade.*

The next step in the progress of our investigations in respect to the relations of the mother-country to the Colonies is to ascertain under what laws the Colonies have grown up and what privileges they now enjoy. At common law a broad distinction is made between a conquered country and a country settled by British

---

* These statistics have been kindly supplied to me by Mr. J. FitzGerald of the Imperial Institute. They have been compiled from the latest returns.

subjects. In the case of a conquered country, the existing law prevails till it is altered by the conqueror. The case of a Colony formed by English settlers is very different. An Englishman, according to Lord Mansfield, on settling in an uncivilised country, carries with him as much of the law of England as is adapted to his situation. Liberty is his birthright, of which he does not divest himself by going to other lands, provided those other lands are not within the jurisdiction of any recognised civilised power. All he requires to complete his status as a Colonist is that the tract of land on which he is settled should be declared by the Home Government to be adopted by them and placed under the protection of the British flag.

In the earlier Colonies the system most in vogue was to grant to any adventurous spirits desirous of settling—for example, in America,—a charter, reserving to the Queen the power of appointing a Governor and creating two Houses of Legislature and committing to the Governor and the two Houses full power to make all laws necessary for the well-being of the new community. In more modern times the usual course has been to appoint during the infancy of a Colony a Governor with a Legislative Assembly, nominated by the Crown, to assist him in the Government; then, as the Colony advances in years, to substitute two Legislative Houses; and, as a last stage, to give responsible government—that is to say, to make the advisers of the Governor responsible to the two Houses in the same manner as the Ministers of the Crown in the United Kingdom are responsible to the two Houses of Parliament.

In granting these institutions to the Colonies, the mother-country has shown no niggard hand, no selfish spirit. She has handed over to them vast tracts of territory—witness her most recent gift of about one million square miles to fifty thousand settlers in Western Australia. She has allowed, contrary to her most cherished policy, her Colonies to raise up against one another the barrier of Protection, and, stranger still, to impose protective duties against goods imported from the mother-country. No advantage, then, has been reserved to the mother-country. She cannot without the consent of the Colony settle her surplus population on lands defended by her navy. She cannot carry into a Colonial port the products of Lancashire or Yorkshire, the results of the industry of their British fellow-subjects, without paying a heavy duty.

What, then, is the position of the Colonist as compared with that of an Englishman, Scotsman, or Irishman—say of a citizen of New South Wales as compared with that of a citizen of Manchester? How do they stand as regards the mother-country? Both are subjects of Her Majesty—as fully as if both had been born in England; they can alike be elected to Parliament, enter the army or navy or be admitted to the bar or to any other profession or calling for which British citizenship is a necessary qualification. Both, wherever they go, can claim the protection of the British Ambassador and the British Consul. Then, as to their powers of government. First, as to local affairs, the New South Wales man has the advantage over the Manchester man: the latter can by his representatives take part in the local government of England, but he has no reserve stock of land with which he can deal sufficient to give many cows and many acres to any of his neighbours who may require them. While in addition to his acres the New South Wales man has, to say the least, as large a power over the local government of his Colony as the Manchester man has over English local government.   Then, as to taxes—the Manchester man belongs to a community which contributes, according to Sir John Colomb, 19s. 5$\frac{3}{4}$d. out of every pound spent on the navy, and 20s. in the pound to the maintenance of the Foreign Office, or, in other words, to the maintenance of the relations of the Empire with foreign countries.   In the benefit of this expenditure the New South Wales citizen has as large a share as the Manchester man, yet what does he contribute?—6$\frac{1}{4}$d. of every pound spent on the navy, nothing to the army, nothing to the Foreign Office expenditure.

Such are the general conditions of the British Empire. It has cost hundreds of millions to build it up—an expense wholly borne by the mother-country.   It costs over 14 millions a year to defend it at sea—the whole of which is defrayed by the British tax-payer, except to the extent of £381,000, of which India pays £254,000, chiefly for troopships and harbours, and Australia the remainder to maintain a local squadron.   It has cost us a blood-tax which can only be estimated by the reflection that, according to some historians, our wars for the last two hundred years have really been sustained for the maintenance, expansion, and consolidation of our Colonial Empire—" Gare à qui la touche."

What, then, are the inducements for the members of this great family to stand by and assist each other and the mother-country, and for the mother-country to keep under her wing these great and growing communities? In considering this question, India is, of course, excluded: it has been won by the sword—it will, if the

necessity arises, of which there appears to be little probability, be kept by the sword; and the considerations
applicable to such a possession are totally distinct from
those which bear on the question of the situation of our
Colonies, properly so-called. The spheres of influence in
Africa and the mere Dependencies are also obviously
excluded.

Some forty years ago a Colonial Society was formed
in London for the purpose of determining the true relations between the mother-country and the Colonies.
All the various political parties were represented amongst
its members. These included Mr. Walpole, Mr. Adder-
ley (now Lord Norton), Sir William Molesworth, Mr.
Cobden, Mr. Godley, one of the founders of the Canter-
bury Settlement in New Zealand, Mr. Bright, and
others. The object of the Society was to obtain self-
government for the greater Colonies, then writhing and
uneasy under the eccentric rule of the Colonial Office
of the day. With this view, the opportunity was taken
by Sir William Molesworth, on the occasion of a Bill
being brought into Parliament in 1850 for the government of the Australian Colonies, to propose a scheme
for conferring on them a complete system of self-government. This proposal, as might be expected, was not
carried. The Government plan prevailed, and these
Colonies did not obtain responsible government till
three or four years later. The principles, however, on
which the Society acted are at this distance of time of
more importance than the mode in which it sought to
carry these principles into effect. It was assumed that
Colonies were outlets for the surplus population of
Great Britain, that it was the duty of the mother-country
to fill up the waste places of the World, and that she

was bound to protect her Colonies so long as they were young and unable to protect themselves, but that national children, like the children of a well-ordered family, should be brought up with a desire to maintain themselves, and that they would, when adult, separate from their parent and set up for themselves. It was taught by the political economists of the time that Free Trade was about to make the World a universal brotherhood, and that the fact of a country being a Colony or not mattered nothing as respected the extent of its commercial intercourse with the mother-country, and that the burden of protecting it as a Colony far outweighed in a financial point of view any possible advantages to be derived by the mother-country from maintaining the connection.

Since 1850 far other counsels have prevailed. "The millennium" of Free Trade has not been established; and, in the event of a war, grave inconveniences would arise to Great Britain, if Australia, for instance, were an independent State. In such an event Australia, however friendly, would be bound by the obligations of a neutral Power. As a belligerent, Great Britain could not fit or refit her ships at any Australian port. She could not obtain supplies, and would have to acknowledge the territorial waters of Australia as a place of refuge within which she could not attack any ship of the enemy.

Again, when the Colonist asserts his desire for independence, has he ever considered that, though not wholly independent, he is in no sense dependent on the mother-country? The British Parliament has long since renounced the power of taxing the Colonies, and all that the mother-country asks of her children, even in case of war, is sympathy and voluntary support. Apart, then, from the higher considerations of feeling and patriotism which, as will be shown hereafter, condemn absolutely the education by the mother-country of her children with a view to separation, it may be admitted that, taking a lower ground, and looking to the protection of our commerce in time of war, every inhabitant of the United Kingdom should desire to retain the affections of his Colonial fellow-subjects by any reasonable concession. In discussing in those bygone years the advantages conferred by a Colony on the mother-country, it never occurred to the philanthropists of the Colonial Society that there existed a possibility of the Colony aiding the mother-country by troops or ships. The possibility of the presence of an Australian Contingent under the British commander in Egypt would have seemed to them a mere dream unworthy of the consideration of any one but a visionary sentimentalist.

If, however, we proceed to weigh in the balance the benefit to the colony as compared with that to the mother-country, which is secured by their mutual connection, it will be seen that the advantages in favour of the colony greatly preponderate. Take Australia as an example, and assume her to be independent. Where would she stand in the commonwealth of nations? Three millions of people would be charged with the protection of 8800 miles of seaboard. How long would Australia be for the Australians? What is there to prevent Germans, Frenchmen, Italians from creating their "spheres of influence" in Australia? England protects them with an expenditure of 14 millions a year, with a fleet that can follow an enemy into every sea, and blockade an enemy in its own ports. What possible force could

Australia raise which could shut up the fleet of any European Power in port, or be prepared to meet such a force in the open sea? Again, in case of separation, at the very time when money was imperatively required for defence, what would be the value of Australian securities? At the present moment the Australian Colonies raise money in the English market at the rate of three and a half per cent. Let them become independent, and great would be the downfall in Australian credit.

If we add to the cost of naval defence the expense of keeping up an army, and last—not least—the cost of a Foreign Office, with Ministers and Consuls and all the attendant paraphernalia of intercourse with Foreign States, it must be admitted that the Australian Republic would scarcely start on its course of independence in these days of annexation and filibustering without casting "a longing, lingering look" at the Old Country and its ever-present, ever-protecting flag. Then, as is well put by Sir John Colomb, and also by Mr. Hervey in his very interesting article, what influence would the Ministers and Consuls of an Australian Republic have? Instead of their Consul being the one to whom foreigners are often glad to apply for assistance, they would be liable in times of danger to find themselves in the position of those foreigners, and to have to appeal to the charity of the British Consul, whose protection they could no longer invoke as a right.

Having, I hope, proved that the views of 1850 were a mistake, and that no English politician of these days would desire to separate the sticks which are unbreakable while bound together, but which would snap so readily were they attacked singly, let us turn to the

L.

problem presented for solution—namely, the formation
within the Empire of a Britannic Confederation. The
phrase "*within* the Empire" is deliberately used; for
it seems sometimes to be forgotten that, assuming the
existence of such a Confederation, no inconsiderable
portion of the Empire—notably India with its population of 286 millions, and the African spheres of influence
—must inevitably be left out.   Moreover, in considering the question in the only form in which it can arise
in the immediate future, we may further narrow its
scope by confining our argument to the larger Colonies
—Canada, Australia, the Cape, and New Zealand; for
any scheme applicable to them can readily be adapted to
the smaller British Possessions when occasion arises.

What, then, is the nature of the proposed Britannic
Confederation which is intended to draw closer the
bonds of union between the mother-country and the
Anglo-Saxon Colonies?   What examples can be found
in contemporary history of forms of government binding
together political communities having local self-governing powers?—for to such forms of government the ex-
pressions " Federation " and " Confederation " are alone
applicable.

An example which may be taken to illustrate all the
characteristics of Federal Union will be found in
the United States Republic.   The thirteen American
Colonies which revolted against British rule, found
themselves at the conclusion of the war in the position
of thirteen independent States, having no connection
with each other.   The common tie of British supremacy
had been dissolved; and each State possessed the prerogatives of making peace and war, of maintaining
armies and navies, of regulating commerce and making

treaties with foreign nations, which had previously been vested in the Sovereign of Great Britain.   Such a state of things was intolerable.   A cluster of thirteen small independent States lay at the mercy of any foreign Power ; and, to obviate this danger, they agreed to form a Confederacy.   This they attempted to do by the establishment of a central body called Congress, consisting of delegates from the component States, and invested with all the prerogatives of the British Crown. The expenses incurred by the Confederacy were to be defrayed out of a common fund, to be supplied by requisitions made on the several States.   The defects of this Confederacy soon became apparent.   Congress was utterly devoid of all coercive authority to carry its laws into effect.   " Every breach of the laws involved a state of war, and military execution became the only instrument of civil obedience." *   "A still more striking defect was the total want of power to lay and levy taxes or to raise revenue to defray the ordinary expenses of government.   Requisitions were to be made on thirteen independent States.   The consequence was that, though in theory the resolutions of the Federal Government were constitutionally binding on the members of the Union, yet in practice they were mere recommendations which the States regarded or disregarded at their option."   Story sums up the whole question as follows : —"It has been justly observed that 'a government authorised to declare war, but relying on independent States for the means of prosecuting it, capable of contracting debts and of pledging the public faith for their payment, but depending on thirteen distinct sovereignties for the preservation of that faith, could

* *Federalist*, p. 74.

only be rescued from ignominy and contempt by finding those sovereignties administered by men exempt
from the passions incident to human nature'—that
is, supposing a case in which all human government
would become unnecessary and all difference of opinion
would become impossible."* In this state of things
the Americans perceived that it was quite possible to
maintain complete unity as a nation if, in addition to
investing the supreme government with the prerogative
powers, they added full power to impose Federal taxes
on the component States and established an executive
furnished with ample means to carry all Federal powers
into effect through the medium of Federal officers. A complete system of Federal taxation enforced by Federal
courts supplied the central government with the necessary funds to perform effectually all the functions of a
supreme national government.

To understand this system it is only necessary to
reflect that every inhabitant of the United States has a
double political status. He belongs to one great nation
called the United States. He is also a citizen of a local
self-governing body called a State.

The Empire of Germany is a Federal Union differing
from the United States of America in having an Emperor
at its head. The King of Prussia, under the title of German Emperor, represents the Empire in all its relations
with foreign nations, and has the prerogative of making
peace and war; but, if the war be more than a defensive
war, he must have the assent of the Upper House.

In considering the position of the Empire and the
prospects of Britannic Confederation, the first reflection
that occurs is that a Britannic Confederation can extend

* Story, chap. ii. p. 96.

only to the Colonies and not to the Imperial Dependencies—meaning by the Colonies, as has been already explained, the settlements of British, or at all events of British and other European, settlers, while the expression Imperial Dependencies is used to designate India, Ceylon, and the countries inhabited in the main by dark-skinned races.   To draw an accurate line of demarcation between these two classes of Colonies and Imperial Dependencies is not possible or necessary.   Again, to enumerate the Settlements included within the category of Colonies would conduce little to the solution of the problem before us, as it is with the typical representatives of each class, and not with details, that we have to deal.   The only fact which it may be well to remember is that the Imperial Dependencies have a population of some 300 millions and a volume of trade of £196,000,000, while the Colonies have a population of some 20 millions and a trade of £162,000,000.   It is not, of course, intended by this comparison to put the Imperial Dependencies on a par with the Colonies in the estimation of Englishmen, but to show the vast numbers whose happiness is involved in the government of the Empire, and the great national interests affected by that government. Now, the common link between the United Kingdom, its Colonies, and its Imperial Dependencies—in other words, the force which makes the Empire—is the sovereignty of the United Kingdom : the prerogative of Her Majesty to make peace and war, to maintain fleets and armies, and to govern by that prerogative alone the Imperial Dependencies.

Let us now consider what privileges the Colonists desire of which they are not already possessed.   They do not, of course, claim to interfere in the local government of the United Kingdom, inasmuch as the British Government does not interfere in their local affairs; and a Canadian or Victorian has, to say the least, as large a power of governing Canada or Victoria as a Yorkshireman has of governing England. Again, the Colonist has little to desire with respect to the regulation of commerce. A citizen of New York or Florida cannot, as such, impose any custom duties or interfere with trade. A citizen of Canada or New South Wales can deal with the import and export of goods into his own Colony as he wills, even to the extent of imposing burdensome duties on the manufactures of the mother-country. It is true, a Colonist cannot make treaties with a foreign country: but to grant this privilege would enable Canada with four millions of inhabitants, or New South Wales with one million, to legislate for the Colonies and Dependencies alike—in other words, to make treaties binding on 303 millions of peoples. Such a concession is obviously out of the question. Again, with respect to the power of making peace or war. The Australians complained some little time ago that we were unwilling to allow the annexation of certain islands in the Pacific. Those islands were of no consequence viewed in relation to the Empire, and their annexation might have involved us in a European war. Would it be right that, for an indirect benefit to a particular Colony or Colonies, a war should be set on foot which would have disturbed the whole Empire and cost thousands of lives and millions of money? And how would a Colony in such a case be benefited by independence? Would all Australia, having a population of only three millions, if she made a demand on any of the great European Powers, have a chance of sustaining that demand? It is sometimes suggested that a Colony may be drawn into war by the mother-country, and would be safer if independent. Here, if ever, the *tu quoque* argument applies. As has been stated above, the Empire is a structure which has cost hundreds of millions of money and millions of lives to erect and maintain. "Where is the woman?" is the question of the wise man, in searching for the origin of any quarrel between individuals: "Where is the Colony?" would be an equally apposite question in respect of any difference arising between Great Britain and any civilised nation. Were Great Britain assisted in the protection of her Colonial Possessions by a Colonial fleet, and of her Indian countries by a native fleet, would she not be a Power capable of defying the nations of the World?

Something may also be said of the vast influence she would possess if her children, following her example, would abolish their hostile tariffs, and adopt Free Trade throughout the Empire. Would not such an Empire be far preferable to any *Zollverein* formed on the impossible lines of a protective tariff imposed by the mother-country on all Colonial products to the detriment of herself and foreign countries? Is it to be expected that the British citizen, who pays so much to maintain the army and navy under the shadow of which the commerce of the Colonies, including their protective tariffs, is carried on, would consent to be further taxed for the benefit of his richer brother in Canada or Australia?

Is it conceivable that Britain, having led the vanguard in Free Trade, should waver in her advance, give up her commercial treaties with foreign countries, and reverse her policy of the last thirty years? Surely it

is more reasonable that the Colonies should substitute
Free Trade for Protection, than to expect that the mother-
country should return to a policy which she abandoned
for the benefit of the working-man, for the advantage
of the very class who, having emigrated, have, contrary
to the opinion of the old Roman poet, changed their
opinions with their change of climate. In short, it is
easier for countries whose united commerce amounts to
160 millions to alter their commercial regulations, than
for Great Britain to risk its 750 millions of trade by
again subjecting it to trammels from which it has been
so lately emancipated.

No argument is required to show that, as the British
Empire exceeds in extent every other union of States
which the World has ever seen, so it presents a complexity of interests which has no parallel in history.

Confederation and Imperial taxation must go hand in
hand. If the Colonies desire representation in an Imperial Parliament they must be prepared to take their
share in all Imperial burdens, including the National
Debt. Further, taxes for Imperial purposes would have
to be collected by Imperial officers and enforced by Imperial courts, as taxes for Federal purposes are levied in
the United States by Federal officers. Such a scheme
of union cannot be looked upon as feasible within the
near future, but must be developed gradually, and progress with the advance of the Colonies in respect of
population and wealth.

But admitting this to be a barrier to the formulation
to-day or to-morrow of a detailed scheme of Confederation,
may we not initiate a system calculated to lead up to
such a union? The problem is a new one : new conditions
require new political relations : and, without attempting

to prophesy what the British Empire may become before the close of another half-century, let us consider what may be done immediately in the way of Britannic Confederation.

Let, as Sir John Colomb suggests, an Imperial army and an Imperial navy, as contradistinguished from a British army and navy, be established by the mother-country, and a fixed status in that army and navy be offered on certain conditions to every Colony. Take first the army, and let me illustrate my meaning by supposing Canada to respond to the invitation of Great Britain. Canada would raise a body of troops and maintain them. They would not be *compelled* to serve in the Imperial army unless Canada were attacked by an enemy of Great Britain: in such an event they would be as completely under the command of Her Majesty's officers as the British troops. In time of peace they would be regulated by the law of the Colony. If the Canadian troops were required for service out of their own country, it would be necessary to obtain their own consent. Form a navy on similar conditions. The ships would be commissioned by Her Majesty, but they would not be required to serve out of a certain restricted area except with their own consent. What has been said of Canada applies to every other Colony desirous of becoming a member of a Britannic Confederation. Let the Colonies contribute in proportion to their size and wealth to the Imperial army and navy, and there can be little doubt that their influence in making peace and war will be in proportion to the strength of their battalions and the number of their ships. Nor need the intervention of the Colonies in British politics be only indirect. The direct intervention of a Colony may be secured by elevating the position of an Agent-General to one more akin to that of a Minister of a Foreign State, and giving him a facility of access to the British Government and a social position commensurate with the important duties with which he would be entrusted.

Social links, as they may be called, between the mother-country and the Colonies might also be multiplied by adopting, as Sir John Colomb proposes, freer postage, telegraphic, and other communications. There seems also no reason why a scheme should not be adopted whereby an interchange should take place between the Civil Service of a Colony and the English Civil Service. The Colonial Office might thus obtain a practical knowledge of genuine Colonial wants and ideas, and the staff of the greater Colonies might be strengthened by the assistance of men versed in the business of the higher departments in the English Civil Service. No stronger argument for the introduction of such a plan can be found than in the career of Sir Robert Herbert, who has just retired from the Colonial Office, to the regret alike of the Colonies and the mother-country. The personal knowledge and experience of Colonial affairs which he gained during his tenure of office as Premier of Queensland from 1860 to 1865 have, by universal consent, given him a unique position as adviser to the Secretary of State for the Colonies.

A material step in advance has already been taken in the blending of English and Colonial ideas by the establishment of the Imperial Institute, whereby Colonists, on their arrival in this country, will find an institution in which they can conveniently meet for business or pleasure and obtain information. Last, but not least, the Imperial Federation League, through its able lecturer, Mr. Parkin, has diffused throughout the United Kingdom and the Colonies a greater knowledge of the advantages to be derived from closer acquaintance and mutual confidence.

What, then, is the outcome of the whole question? The Colonies have all the powers of government, which communities can possess, except the Sovereign's prerogative of making peace and war and regulating commerce with foreign nations. These powers are, both in monarchical and republican States, vested in the head of the supreme government, and are practically controlled in constitutional States by the necessity of appealing to the people for money to carry on a war or for laws to enforce treaties. If the Colonists are desirous of making their influence felt on these questions, the means are in their own hands. Let them ask the mother-country to form an Imperial army and navy, and let them contribute their quota to the land forces and reinforce the navy with their ships. As they grow in strength they will grow in influence, and when the five millions of Canadians have become a hundred millions, when the Australians can reckon fifty instead of three million inhabitants, and their local naval and military forces have grown in equal proportion, it may be that their numbers may be so great as to virtually shift the supremacy from the old country to the new; but that time has not yet arrived. The immediate Britannic Confederation should consist of a political organisation in which the Queen should maintain the existing prerogatives, but in which the Colonies, who are able and willing to give substantial assistance in the defence of the Empire, should be represented in London by Ministers, as suggested above.

Let me not be misunderstood. We may attempt
"to dip into the future as far as human eye can see,"
and imagine an ideal State with its millions of British
subjects commanding such an ascendancy in the World
as to be able to insist that—

> "The war-drum throb no longer and the battle-flag be furled
> In the Parliament of man, the Federation of the World;"

but the hour is not yet, and for the present we must
rest the stability of the Empire on the mutual affection
of the mother-country and her vast Colonial family.
What is there wanting in such a tie? There is a common
origin, a common flag, a community of glorious recollec-
tions. The Canadian, the Australian, the New Zea-
lander, each has his share in Agincourt, in Blenheim, in
Waterloo, in the Crimea; his fathers were Englishmen—he, too, is an Englishman. "*Civis Romanus sum.*"
"I am a British subject," he may proclaim everywhere,
and he will find his claim allowed and respected. It
may be said that such ties are merely sentimental,
silken ties, broken by the slightest strain. If this be
so, then love of country is a mere sentiment, nationality
is a mere sentiment—the purest, liveliest, strongest
affections of the human heart are mere sentiments.
History tells us in every page that a common nationality
is the firmest bond which unites men in political communities. Look abroad at Poland, still restless and
uneasy because her nationality has been crushed and
trampled upon. Consider the Slav aspiration for unity,
seething and disturbing Europe with its misplaced
energy and ambitious cravings. Ask the Hungarian
why he revolted from Austria and is content because his
nationality is recognised. Search the World throughout

its length and breadth, and it will be found that com-
binations of States are strong and compact in proportion as their component members possess a common
nationality and are bound together by a community of
sentiment. Great Britain and her Colonies are the
greatest combination of States of a similar origin which
the World has yet known. They are held together by
the firmest tie—that of "kindred blood, similar privileges, and equal protection."

THRING.

INDEX.

GEORGE PHILIP AND SON, LONDON AND LIVERPOOL.